Microsoft Teams

Bible

Microsoft Teams

Bible

By

Jason Taylor

TABLE OF CONTENTS

4

5

6

8

9

Jason Taylor

INTRODUCTION

In an increasingly digital world, the way we communicate and collaborate has transformed dramatically. The shift from traditional office environments to remote and hybrid work models has accelerated the need for effective communication tools that foster collaboration, enhance productivity, and streamline workflows. Enter Microsoft Teams—a powerful platform designed to meet the challenges of modern teamwork.

Microsoft Teams is more than just a chat application; it's a comprehensive hub for teamwork that integrates seamlessly with Microsoft 365 applications and services. Launched in 2017, Teams has quickly become a cornerstone for organizations seeking to enhance their communication strategies and improve team collaboration. With features that support chat, video conferencing, file sharing, and project management, Teams empowers users to work together efficiently, regardless of their physical location.

As businesses worldwide adapt to new realities, the importance of effective collaboration tools cannot be overstated. Remote work has become the norm, and teams are often spread across different geographical locations and time zones. This presents unique challenges in maintaining

11

communication, aligning goals, and fostering a sense of belonging among team members. Microsoft Teams addresses these challenges head-on, providing a versatile platform that enables seamless interaction and collaboration.

THE EVOLUTION OF WORK

The traditional workplace has evolved significantly over the past few decades, driven by technological advancements and changing workforce dynamics. The rise of digital communication tools has transformed how teams interact, making it possible to connect instantly, share information, and collaborate in real time. However, with so many tools available, many organizations face the challenge of managing disparate systems that can lead to confusion and inefficiency.

Microsoft Teams aims to simplify this landscape by offering a unified platform that consolidates various communication methods—instant messaging, voice calls, video conferencing, and file sharing—into one cohesive environment. This integration not only enhances communication but also promotes a culture of collaboration where teams can work together more effectively.

WHY MICROSOFT TEAMS?

The need for effective collaboration tools has never been more evident. As organizations face the challenges of remote work, the ability to connect, engage, and collaborate in real-time is crucial. Microsoft Teams addresses these needs with its robust set of features that promote seamless communication and teamwork. Let's explore some of the key reasons why Microsoft Teams has become a preferred choice for organizations:

- **Unified Communication**: Teams brings together various communication methods into a single platform. This eliminates the need for multiple applications, streamlining workflows and enhancing productivity. Users can easily switch between chat, calls, and meetings without losing context or momentum.

- **Integration with Microsoft 365**: One of Teams' strongest advantages is its deep integration with other Microsoft 365 tools. This enables users to access files from OneDrive, collaborate in real-time on Word and Excel documents, and manage projects using Planner—all within the Teams interface. This interconnectedness makes it easier for teams to access the resources they need without switching between different platforms.

13

- **Customizable Experience**: Teams offers a flexible and customizable environment. Users can create channels tailored to specific projects or topics, use apps and bots to enhance functionality, and personalize notifications to stay informed on important updates. This adaptability allows teams to mold the platform to fit their unique workflows and preferences.
- **Security and Compliance**: With built-in security features and compliance tools, Teams ensures that your communications and data remain secure. Organizations can trust that their information is protected, meeting industry standards and regulations. This is particularly crucial in industries that handle sensitive data, as Microsoft Teams provides robust security measures to safeguard information.
- **Enhancing Team Culture**: In the age of remote work, maintaining a positive team culture is essential. Microsoft Teams provides features that foster social interaction and team bonding, such as the ability to create fun polls, share GIFs, and celebrate achievements publicly. These elements

14

help to create a sense of community, even in a virtual environment.

WHAT TO EXPECT IN THIS BOOK

In the chapters that follow, we will cover:

- **Getting Started with Teams:** An introduction to the Teams interface, how to set up your account, and basic navigation tips. We'll walk through the initial setup process, ensuring you are comfortable with the platform before diving deeper.
- **Communication Tools:** A deep dive into chat functionalities, video conferencing, and calling features, including best practices for effective virtual meetings. We'll explore how to utilize chat effectively to enhance communication, as well as how to schedule and conduct meetings that engage participants.
- **Collaboration Features:** How to create and manage teams and channels, share files, and collaborate in real-time on documents. You will learn how to set up dedicated spaces for different projects and how to utilize the full suite of collaboration tools available.
- **Integrating Apps and Services:** Exploring how to enhance your Teams experience with third-party

15

apps, bots, and Microsoft 365 integrations. We'll highlight popular integrations and show you how to customize your Teams environment to include the tools your team uses most.

- **Managing Your Teams Environment:** Tips for administrators on configuring settings, managing users, and ensuring a secure and productive environment. This section will be invaluable for those responsible for overseeing Teams usage within their organization.

- **Advanced Features:** Insights into using Teams for project management, automation with Power Automate, and leveraging analytics for better decision-making. We will delve into advanced functionalities that can help teams optimize their workflows and productivity.

THE JOURNEY AHEAD

By the end of this book, you will not only be proficient in using Microsoft Teams but also equipped with strategies to maximize its potential for your organization. You will learn how to foster a culture of collaboration, enhance communication, and ultimately drive productivity within your team.

16

Whether you are a team leader, project manager, or individual contributor, mastering Microsoft Teams will provide you with the skills needed to thrive in today's dynamic work environment. We aim to empower you not just with knowledge, but with practical tools and insights that can be implemented immediately.

As we embark on this journey, remember that effective collaboration is not just about the tools we use; it's about the people behind those tools. Embracing a mindset of collaboration, open communication, and continuous improvement will position you and your team for success. Let's dive into the world of Microsoft Teams and explore how it can transform the way you collaborate, communicate, and create together.

CHAPTER ONE

GETTING STARTED WITH TEAMS

Teams can be accessed through three different channels. There are slightly various restrictions on what you can do with each format that you can access a team in. For instance, you may now access a team using the following methods:

- Your web browser by logging into your Office 365 subscription
- A Windows computer running the Teams client program;
- An iOS (Apple) or Android smartphone running the aforementioned app

Teams can be accessed through certain web browsers, as an app for iPhones, Android phones, or Windows phones, and as an installed client for Mac or Windows desktops. The first thing you'll likely notice is that you have varied features depending on the kind of client you're using. This is essentially an industry standard when comparing a website or Windows client to a smartphone app. The majority of phone apps can't offer as much functionality as other possible application development methods. Most of the time, all platforms have enough features to make the product useful. Just be advised that the product has differences and

18

that, due to its recent introduction to the market, numerous features will continue to be added, modified, or updated for its various customers.

Microsoft's Skype for Business product division created the Journey from Skype Teams. Microsoft Teams will eventually replace Skype for Business, but it's crucial to remember that this is a longer-term goal and won't happen right away. Currently, a long-term supported version of Skype for Business 2019 is still scheduled for release. Microsoft Teams cannot yet be installed on local systems; it is only accessible through the cloud. It's crucial to remember that while Teams can be used with an on-premises installation of Microsoft Exchange (one of Teams' components), several of its functions, like eDiscovery for Teams, are not yet compatible with that setup.

As a quick reference, you must be completely in the cloud on the Office 365 suite and its associated apps (SharePoint, Exchange, Skype for Business, and OneDrive for Business) in order to take advantage of all the capabilities that Teams offers and the new features that are constantly being introduced.

It's also crucial to remember that while Skype for Business served as a foundation for Microsoft Teams, not all of its features are now accessible in Teams. According to the Microsoft roadmap, however, they are in progress and should be delivered in the near future (or have already been provided, depending upon when you are reading this book).

Microsoft Teams is an application that combines several separate programs into one. But for Teams to work, a few essential components are needed. The following things are made in the background on Microsoft's servers outside of Teams each time you create a new team:

- Office 365 Groups (Modern Groups)—unless you add a team and select an already-existing group.
- Exchange Online group mailbox;
- SharePoint site collection (including a document library);

Because these other programs are "masked" behind the Microsoft Teams UI, it may not be immediately obvious that you are utilizing them when using Microsoft Teams. The Files tab on your team is one instance of this. You can see that all of your documents seem to be in Teams. But in reality, they are kept in the background in SharePoint. Although this isn't very important to know as a regular user, if you are the administrator of a Microsoft Teams environment, these are important things to know because

20

some of the maintenance and repairs you do may be done in that program directly rather than through Microsoft Teams.

TEAMS AND SHAREPOINT

A modern SharePoint Online site with a document library is one of the elements that is created when a team is formed. Because SharePoint On-Premises is not supported, your tenant must have SharePoint Online activated in order to use Microsoft Teams. This team creates the shared documents library for you, but if you currently have all of your documents in another location, you can use an existing document library from another SharePoint site.

Take note: Although there is a folder in SharePoint Online for the files you work with that corresponds to each channel in Microsoft Teams, the folder is not created until a file is posted.

This SharePoint document library contains some of the files that users submit "behind the scenes." These documents are stored in a SharePoint document library. Later in this book, we discuss the locations of each file.

USING THE SITE COLLECTION IN SHAREPOINT OUTSIDE OF TEAMS

It's a valid question that relies on your personal logic as to whether or not we should encourage users to use the

21

SharePoint site collection for other purposes (workflows, lists, etc.). The Shared Documents folder is currently the only part of the SharePoint site collection that shows up in Microsoft Teams automatically. Other SharePoint components can be used; however, they must be added as links from a tab or through cloud storage.

In order to get around Teams' current lack of channel-based security, one possible benefit of using the SharePoint site collection outside of the Teams UI is that SharePoint offers far more granular security. However, this has the drawback that you are opening SharePoint and Microsoft Teams to handle separate objects.

Be careful: Changing the folder structure of the channels does not update the channels in Teams, even if you can add other items to a SharePoint site collection to add to the channel tab for convenient access. Only the Teams interface should be used to create them.

TEAMS AND GROUPS

By organizing users into relevant groups, Office 365 Groups (also known as Modern Groups) enables you to configure security or notifications for a variety of apps. An Office 365 group is technically an Azure Active Directory object. It is compatible with the majority of Office 365 apps and can

22

have one or more members. For instance, you might have salespeople in your marketing department. For example, you could make a group named Marketing, add all of the staff members from that department to it, and then add the group to the application or applications you use. Compared to constantly adding each user separately to every program for security and notifications, this is far simpler to administer.

Because an Office 365 group is the parent of a team, it is important to use Office 365 Groups with Microsoft Teams. Unless you choose to build a team from an existing Office 365 group, every time you create a new team, an Office 365 group is created. Additionally, you have the option to make the team secret or public (the group is of the same type). In any event, the security and other elements of your team are managed behind the scenes by a higher-level organization. As we delve deeper into Teams administration later in the book, the connection between Office 365 Groups and Teams becomes even more crucial. For the time being, just know that one of the numerous components ensuring the smooth operation of your team is an Office 365 group.

TEAMS AND EXCHANGE/OUTLOOK

Exchange only makes all of its features available when it is completely online within the Office 365 suite, just like other

23

Office 365 apps with which Microsoft Teams communicates. While Exchange On-Premises and Exchange Dedicated (old) can be used with Microsoft Teams, some features are functionally compatible while others are not. Note: All of Microsoft Teams' functionalities are available to users hosted on Exchange Online or Exchange Dedicated Next.

The main point is that Microsoft Teams creates a group mailbox using Exchange to hold team data, including meetings (messages are kept in a SharePoint folder). Depending on your version of Exchange, you can check which features are active or disabled by going to the Microsoft website at https://docs(dot)microsoft(dot)com/en-us/microsoftteams/exchange-teams-interact.

Take note: Every user should be able to create Office 365 Groups, Exchange Online, and SharePoint Online in order to fully utilize Microsoft Teams.

ONEDRIVE FOR TEAMS AND BUSINESS
Microsoft Teams makes use of OneDrive for Business. It is mostly used to store shared files from team chats (not channel conversations). Only the designated user can view the files because permissions are automatically limited.

PUTTING TOGETHER A TEAM
To form a team:

24

- Click Add team, which is situated in the Teams app's lower left corner.
- Press the button to create a team.
- Type in the team's name, description, and privacy preferences.
- Increase the number of team members. You can choose a distribution list, a person's name, or a mail-enabled security group.

Make sure the team has a meaningful name. Although it is optional, it is encouraged to enter a description for the team. A description assists members of the organization in deciding which public team to join as more and more teams are introduced. You must also choose how to handle the new team's privacy. Private is the default setting if you don't modify it. This implies that team members can only be added by team owners. Additionally, a team can be made public,

25

allowing anyone in the company with a Microsoft Teams license to join.

It's crucial to confirm that there isn't already a team with the name you intend to use. There is nothing stopping you from giving your team the same name as another, but doing so may cause confusion and other problems for your users. Making a team out of an existing Office 365 group is an additional choice. To begin building a new team, click the **"Join or create a team"** option at the bottom of the window. Click the **"Create a team"** button after that. After that, a window with the option to **"Create a team from an existing Office 365 group"** will open. A list of the groups you own is presented to you for selection. The team can be formed after the group has been chosen. Every individual who is a member of the group is added to the team.

Drag & drop teams into the desired location to rearrange them in the left menu. It moves the channels that are a component of the team.

OVERSEEING A TEAM
Only a small range of options are provided to define the parameters of a newly created team. The Manage team option is used for a lot of this. You have the ability to modify the team's general settings for each member within this

section. This involves establishing the general permissions for both internal and external users. Additionally, you can alter the team image (icon) and decide whether @mentions and entertaining elements like emojis or animated GIFs are permitted.

Let's go over how to include a picture of the squad.

- Choose Manage team after clicking the ellipse (...) next to the team's name.
- After choosing the Settings tab, pick the team photo. Extend the section. Choose the image by clicking the "Change picture" link. Find the image you wish to use in the pop-up box.
- Press the Save icon.

EDITING A GROUP

There may be circumstances in which a team's name or description needs to be changed, such as organizational changes, the emergence of another team with the same name inside your business, or feedback from team members.

HOW TO CHANGE THE NAME OF A TEAM

- Click the ellipse (...) next to the team's name, and then choose Edit team.
- Modify the privacy settings, team name, and description as needed.

27

- Press the button marked "Done."

HOW TO INCLUDE MEMBERS OF THE TEAM

Members of both private and public teams can be added by team owners. To increase the number of team members:

- Click the ellipse (...) to the right of the name, and then choose Add members.
- To add a person, distribution list, or mail-enabled security group to the team, start typing their name.
- Press the Add button.
- A notice email confirming their inclusion on the team will be sent to the individuals you add.

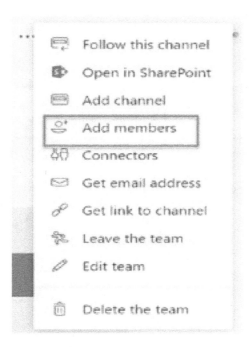

29

DELETING A TEAM

All channels, chats, files, and the Office 365 group are erased when a team is removed. When a team is destroyed, it is said to be in a "soft-delete" state and is stored in the tenant's "recycle bin" in Azure Active Directory (AAD) for 30 days. PowerShell can be used to restore the team during this period; however, an administrator is needed. A deleted team may not resurface for up to 24 hours following restoration.

However, the team is permanently erased from the environment once 30 days have gone by without being recovered, and nobody—not even Microsoft—can get it back.

HOW TO DELETE A TEAM

- Click the ellipsis (…) next to the team's name, and then choose Delete the team.
- Select the checkbox acknowledging that everything has been erased.
- Press the button to delete the team.

Office 365 Groups are occasionally utilized for objectives unrelated to Microsoft Teams. The team cannot be removed, but the group can be kept for other uses.

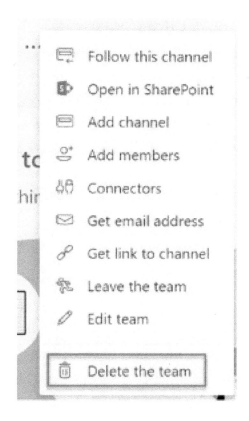

CHAPTER TWO

THE CHANNELS

Teams can divide information and discussions for various projects, topics, companies, or disciplines by using channels. Every IT project at one of the companies we worked with had its own team. They established channels for various project work activities, including development, quality assurance, and project management, within those teams. In the application navigation, the channels are positioned beneath the teams while viewing them. Every team member has access to every channel.

A channel's membership cannot be different from that of the team it belongs to. any piece of material in any channel is accessible to team members. Microsoft may eventually provide a feature that would enable securing channels for specific users, but at the time this book was written, it was not yet available.

HOW TO ADD A CHANNEL

Every team member has the ability to create a channel for the team by default. A General channel is included by default when a team is formed. Content pertaining to the overarching goals and objectives as well as team discussions

32

should be posted on this channel. When working together and talking about a more focused topic,

It is advised to start a new channel. Prior to starting a channel, you should confirm that your intended topic isn't already covered by another channel.

Adding a channel

- Select Add channel by clicking the ellipsis (...) next to the team's name.

- The channel should be given a name and a description.

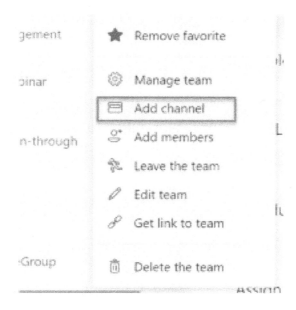

33

When asked to give your channel a name, make sure it's something meaningful. Entering a description for the channel is advised even though it is not required. As a team expands and additional channels are created, descriptions assist team members in figuring out where to communicate and work together. Duplication of channels can also be prevented with a sensible channel name and description. Another team member might make a channel with comparable discussions and content if the name is unfamiliar and there is no description.

HOW TO MANAGE A CHANNEL

It could be necessary to alter the channel's name or description as the discussions and content inside it change. To change the name or description of the channel

- Select Edit this channel after clicking the ellipse (…) next to the channel name.
- Modify the description or name of the channel.
- Select "Save."

HOW TO DELETE A CHANNEL

The need to remove a channel will inevitably arise during an organization's Microsoft Teams adoption process. It's possible that someone will inadvertently create a channel or try to create one without really needing one because any team member can do so by default. For instance, a channel might be made for a subject that already has one active. The channel with the least amount of content in this situation ought to be removed. Reaching the channel limit is another situation that results in deletion. Each team can only have a maximum of 200 channels. 200 channels ought to be more than sufficient for the majority of teams, but if the maximum is drawing near, it might be essential to remove channels that are rarely or never used. All tabs and discussions are erased along with the channel when it is deleted. It is possible to restore the channel, however it cannot be recreated with the same name as a new one. This implies that while you can restore a channel you've erased, you won't be able to use the same channel name again.

To remove a channel:

- Select "Delete this channel" after clicking the ellipse (...) next to the channel name.
- Click the Delete button.
- You are given a URL to the folder containing the channel files when you delete a channel. The files are not erased when the channel is deactivated since they are saved in SharePoint.

35

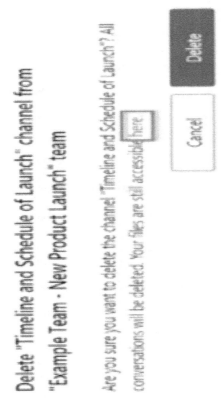

Delete "Timeline and Schedule of Launch" channel from "Example Team - New Product Launch" team

Are you sure you want to delete the channel "Timeline and Schedule of Launch"? All conversations will be deleted. Your files are still accessible here

Cancel   Delete

HOW TO DELETE CHANNEL FILES

- Choose the Files tab after navigating to the General channel.
- In SharePoint, click Open. This displays a glimpse of the channel folder in your web browser's team document library.

36

- To the left of the channel name, select Documents.
- Select Delete after selecting the checkmark to the left of the channel name folder.

HOW TO RESTORE A CHANNEL

The restore channel feature makes it easy to rapidly restore a deleted channel if necessary.

To get a channel back:

- Choose Manage team after clicking the ellipse (...) next to the team's name.
- Choose the tab for Channels. The deleted section displays any channels that have been removed.
- Select "Restore."

CHANNEL EMAIL

An email address is included with every channel. A new Teams chat thread is created when the channel is emailed. At the beginning of the chat, the email address of the sender is displayed. The email body comes after the topic, which is bolded and displayed first. Additionally, a link to the initial email is provided.

This is available to all members of the organization but not to outside visitors. The email opens in Outlook when you click on that link. The user is prompted to log into Outlook

37

if they are not already. Every email communication is stored in the channel folder's Emails subfolder. The purpose of this channel email feature is to prevent crucial messages from getting lost in interminable email chains. When someone replies to an email without remembering to Reply All or passes it to another person, individuals frequently overlook important information. These mistakes can be avoided with the help of the channel email. Additionally, being able to browse past channel chats makes it much easier to acquaint new team members with the system. To obtain the email address of the channel

- Click Get email address after selecting the ellipse (…) next to the channel name.
- Click the Copy button.

Links to the advanced settings and to delete the email address are shown next to the email address. The system generates the email address, which is unchangeable. The email address can be swiftly copied and pasted into an email by using the Copy button. By selecting the advanced options link, you may manage who can send emails to the channel email address. By default, a channel email address is open to everybody, including those who are not affiliated with the team or organization. You can specify that emails can only

38

be sent from specific domains or that only team members can email the channel email address. A few examples of email domains are @melihubb.com, @hotmail.com, @gmail.com, and @noteworthytt.com. Clicking the "Remove email address" button disables the email address. A delivery failure message will appear if someone attempts to email the channel after an email address has been deleted.

The channel email address cannot be restored once it has been deleted. If you are certain that you do not want the channel email address feature, then delete the email.

CHANNEL CONNECTION

In certain situations, you might wish to recommend a channel to someone who hasn't used Microsoft Teams yet and is unsure of what a channel is or where to locate one. Additionally, an organization's members may belong to multiple teams, each of which may have a variety of channels. Here, all you have to do is send a team member the channel's link, which they can then paste into their web browser. After that, customers are given the option to access the channel in the browser or, if they have the Teams app installed, to open it in the app. A non-team member will not be allowed to access the channel if they attempt to utilize the

39

connection.

HOW TO OBTAIN THE URL TO THE CHANNEL

- Click Get a link to the channel after selecting the ellipse (…) next to the channel name.
- Press the Copy icon.

HOW TO SELECT A CHANNEL YOU LIKE

Team members can follow and favorite channels to stay up to date on the discussions and material in a channel. The channel name appears in the list beneath the team's name when a member favorites a channel. To access a channel that isn't favorited, the user must click on more channels beneath the final favorited channel in the list. Every person who has favorited a channel gets notified when it is @mentioned in a conversation. The five most popular channels are automatically favorited when a new team member is added. When a new channel is formed, it is immediately added to the favorites list if there are fewer than five channels.

How to mark a channel as a favorite:

- Click the arrow next to additional channels beneath the team's name.
- To the right of the channel name, click the star.

HOW TO FOLLOW A CHANNEL

Every time a new conversation message is added, the member who is following the channel is notified. Members can observe all recent talks in the channels they are following in the activity feed. Members are advised to follow only the channels that are most important to them. The volume of notifications that are sent out depends on how busy a channel is. If a member follows too many channels, they may tend to ignore the notifications all completely, which render them useless.

To follow a channel:

- Select the channel name by clicking the ellipse (...) adjacent to it.

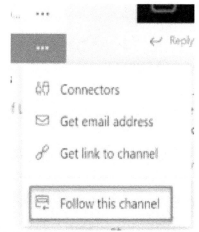

- Follow this channel.

41

Team members can view all of the activity on the channels they follow in the activity feed, along with any mentions of themselves or any team or channel they are a part of. They can see responses to their conversation messages as well as message likes. Additionally displayed are all of the saved discussion messages

CHANNELS MANAGEMENT

A team may monitor and manage all of its channels in a single perspective. This displays the names and descriptions of the channels as well as the number of subscribers. The date of the channel's most recent activity is also visible. You can see how many hours ago the last activity was if it took place on the current day.

To control the channels:

- Select "Manage team" after clicking the ellipsis (…) next to the team's name.
- Select Channels.

TABS

The configurable workspace in Microsoft Teams is made possible via tabs. Tabs are containers inside a team's channels that house content linked to a cloud-based service. Tabs can be used to view and work on files, webpages, SharePoint lists and libraries, Planner tasks, Power BI

42

reports, and even third-party cloud-based apps. Each channel can be customized with its own set of tabs. Every channel comes with three tabs by default: Files, Wiki, and Conversations. Because they are essential components of Microsoft Teams, the Conversations and Files tabs cannot be removed, however the Wiki tab may.

Note: You can expand and view it without the teams and channels list on the left side of the app or the tabs and team name at the top if you want to concentrate on working in just one tab.

TALKS TAB

Within a team, each channel has its own Conversations tab. It is not possible to watch all of the talks that take place in the channels at once. Stated differently, it is not possible to see all team discussions from all channels in a single view.

TAB FOR FILES

Team members can work together and share documents and other materials by uploading them to the materials tab. Only files that are relevant to the channel topic should be added. It is not advisable to save private files on the Files tab. All of the files uploaded in the various channel tabs are stored in a single SharePoint document library for the team, which sets it apart from the Conversations tab. Each channel has its own

43

document library folder. A view of the files in the Channel folder appears when you click the Files tab in a channel. File type, Name, Modified, and Modified by are the fields that are shown. The date that the file was last modified is displayed in the modified field. It indicates how many hours ago the file was modified if this occurred during the last 24 hours. Which team member made the most recent changes to the file is indicated in the Modified by field.

UPLOADING FILES ONLINE

A file can be uploaded to the Files tab.

- Select "Upload."
- Decide which file or files you wish to submit.
- Select "Open."

REMOVING FILES

Using the Files tab to remove a file:

- Click the document to make it blue-highlighted.
- Press the Delete button.
- Select "Confirm."

Take note: A file is transferred to the SharePoint recycle bin when it is deleted from the Files tab.

DOWNLOADING FILES

A file can be downloaded from the Files tab.

44

- Click the document to make it blue-highlighted. 2. Select "Download." The folder containing the downloaded files opens.
- Click Open after selecting the file.

THE WIKI TAB

Ideas and information are rapidly captured on a single central page per channel using the Wiki tab. The Wiki tab is consisting of pages and sections. Pages are shown in a navigation window on the left when you add them. A table of contents-like functionality is created when sections are added to a page and show up in the navigation beneath the page they are a part of.

Organizations can use the wiki page to convey information, such as a checklist or the steps of a process. Each checklist item should have its own section so that team members may debate the process and offer feedback using the built-in discussions feature. New team members can leave comments and offer suggestions, for instance, if you build a wiki page with a checklist of items that must be done when a new employee joins a project. The wiki page is where all of this takes place. In addition to being visible within the wiki page, the talks are also added for visibility within a channel's talks tab. A link in a discussion message directs team members to

45

the wiki page. A response to a conversation in the Conversations tab is also shown in the conversation itself in the relevant wiki section. Additionally, a channel can have more wiki tabs added to it. The SharePoint site collection that is established when you create a team is where the wiki information is kept on the back end. First, a document library called Teams Wiki Data contains all of the channel's wiki content. When you create your first wiki page, the system automatically creates this folder.

Each channel has its own subfolder within the Teams Wiki Data folder. The system files for each wiki are located inside these subfolders. Since every wiki page is saved as a .mht file, it is preferable to edit wikis only in Microsoft Teams rather than using the SharePoint document library.

HOW TO ADD A TAB

To make a tab:

- To the far right of the channel's tabs section, click the + symbol.
- Choose the connector for the service you wish to utilize and connect to in the tab.
- The following step in inserting the tab depends on the connector you choose. You are asked to choose a file

46

or work product, or to create a new one, depending on what you choose.

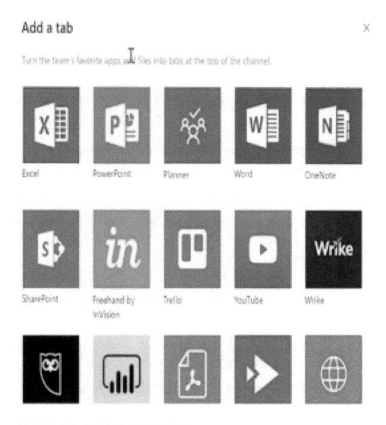

HOW TO REMOVE A TAB

- Select the tab you wish to remove by clicking on its name.
- Click the drop-down arrow and choose Remove.

47

- When prompted, click Remove.
- Although the tab has been removed, the file or work product that is shown has not been removed from the source.

Connectors serve as entry points to cloud services with which Microsoft Teams can communicate. The connectors are located inside the channel's tabs. Numerous Office 365 applications, including Planner, Excel, and OneNote, are compatible with Microsoft Teams. It is also possible to link third-party services like Trello, Twitter, GitHub, and Smartsheet. A web hook can be used to develop bespoke connectors. Microsoft's website has more information about creating custom connectors.

A connector ceases to function until it is recreated by a different team member if the original creator is removed from the group.

HOW TO ADD A CONNECTION

- Select Connectors after clicking the ellipse (…) next to the channel name.
- Search for the desired service and then select the Configure button.
- Enter the service and log in.

48

Keep your group current with content and updates from other services.

Search 🔍

All

Sort by Popularity ▾

MANAGE
Configured
My Accounts

CATEGORY

All
Analytics
CRM
Customer Support
Developer Tools
HR

Connections for your teams

Visual Studio Team Services
Collaborate on and manage software projects online

Configure

RSS
Get RSS feeds for your group

Configure

Incoming Webhook
Send data from a service to your Office 365 group in real time

Configure

JIRA
Gather, organize, and assign issues detected in your software

Configure

Twitter
Send and receive messages called tweets

Configure

49

Keep in mind that a connector is a link to another service that has the ability to read and write data to and from your company. This is somewhat advantageous because it keeps you in the Microsoft Teams application. However, your administrators may consider it a security or data concern. To ensure that only the options approved for your company can be utilized, you can enable or disable each connector independently in the Office 365 administration portal.

Although there are some filtering options, Microsoft Teams' search functionality is a little basic. It is disappointing that Microsoft Teams does not yet offer the rich, sortable, and finely granular search experience that SharePoint offers. The files you deal with must be found through searching, so let's go over the available options and how to make the most of them.

The search experience starts with a combined search and command bar. It should go without saying: simply type the term you're looking for. All of your teams are searched broadly as a result. The following filtering categories contain one or more of the results:

- People
- Files
- Messages

Results from your private chats, emails sent to a team, discussions with bots, and channel talks that are publicly visible within a team channel are all returned by the Messages category. The outcomes from the wiki, meeting titles, or documents on your Files tab—such as those from Google Drive, Dropbox, or OneDrive for Business—are not returned.

To locate individuals within your company, use the People category. Use the Filter tab if you want to locate data from a certain individual. Word, Excel, PowerPoint, OneNote, picture, text, and PDF files are all returned by the Files tab. The search phrase that appears in the filename or body of the text is returned by Teams. Additionally, it looks for materials that contain your search term inside.zip files. You may search across the majority of Teams' components, such as Exchange, SharePoint, and OneDrive for Business, using Content Search. Only administrators who use the Office 365 administration center can access it.

CHAPTER THREE
APPLYING THE SEARCH FILTER

Finding content can get more challenging as teams and the volume of content increase. You can use the Filter tab (pane) to narrow down the search results. Only Messages and Files have the Filter tab; the People category does not have a filter option. You can refine by team, file type, and/or the last person to work on the file.

52

THE COMMAND BAR AND QUICK COMMANDS

The search box is integrated with the command bar. Shortcuts that carry out a task or provide a piece of data are called quick commands. / or @ symbols are used to begin quick commands.

- @commands

You can search within a given context by using @commands. If you are accustomed to using Title:MyWord to search for a word in the title of a web result in Google, the @command is an example of a similar function, but it is used in the context of an installed app or a person (for example, @mentioning someone on Twitter). A list of users and programs that you can use the @command with is displayed when you type the @ sign. The command bar then appears before any search you do with the Weather app once you select the @Weather command. Today, you can look up the weather in cities all across the world.

Take note: You are requested to install the app if you use a @command for one that you do not already have installed.

- /commands

Another method to complete a task or retrieve data fast is to use the shortcuts, often known as slash commands

(/commands), in the command bar. Less than 20 slash commands were accessible to users at the time this book was written. This probably going to rise as Microsoft Teams becomes more and more popular.

The list of available slash commands is as follows:

- /available: Modifies your team's status to Available;
- /away: Modifies your team's status to Away;
- /activity: Views a team member's activity
- /busy: Sets the status of your team to Busy.
- /call: Make a phone call
- /dnd: Sets the status of your team to Do Not Disturb.
- View your most recent files by going to /files. Access a certain team or channel.
- /help: Seek assistance (with Teams, not the "leave the couch" sort).
- Join a team by using /join. View keyboard shortcuts by using /keys.
- /mentions: View every mention you've made (useful if your team's channels are extremely busy!)
- /saved: See your saved list;
- /unread: View all of your unread activities;
- /org: View an org chart (yours or someone else's).
- /whatsnew: View the latest developments in Teams.

54

- /who: Ask Who is a new software that allows you to look for persons by topic or name. A query Some of the more common slash commands are covered in the following.

When you can recall who last worked on a file but not its particular name, /activity /activity aids in finding information. If someone quit your project and you want to see what they were working on recently so you can allocate it to someone else, it can also be helpful. /dnd, /available, /busy, /away /dnd, /available, /busy, and /away provide simple and quick methods for altering your notification status. These commands notify people of your availability by changing the colored icon next to your name, however it might take a few seconds. The /dnd command immediately redirects calls to your voice mail and sets your status to Do Not Disturb. You can see whether you are available or not with the help of the other three slash commands. Unlike the /dnd command, these commands don't stop someone from contacting or messaging you.

WHO?

The Who Bot, which is used to locate specific individuals (and more in-depth details about them) within your company, is activated by the /who command. It asks you to give it permission to do searches on your behalf if you have never used it before.

You are asked to choose the result you are looking for if, for some reason, more than one result comes up. If you receive multiple results from the Who Bot. A card presents further information about the user after you have selected the appropriate person to ask questions about.

Activity-based data, including the individual's manager, peers, and coworkers, can be found from this source. This can be useful, for instance, if you need to find someone who can help you with the duties that person typically performs while they are on leave. Since higher-level executives are typically expected to be treated in a formal manner, you may also use it to find out the person's degree of management before you speak with them. To speed up your work, Teams offers a plethora of additional slash commands. Feel free to try them out for yourself.

Advice

Let's talk about a few brief recommendations to make your working experience even better as we conclude this chapter on how to work effectively in Microsoft Teams.

KEYBOARD SHORTCUTS

Let's start by talking about keyboard shortcuts. By hitting ALT+/ on your keyboard, you can view all of the shortcuts that are accessible. While some of these keyboard shortcuts are unique to Teams and Skype for Business, others are available on Windows. Try a few of them out and see which ones suit you the best.

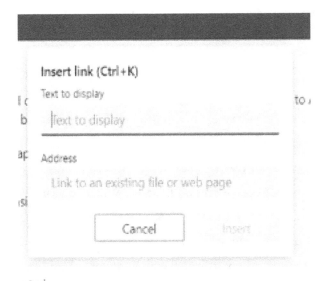

cated

Ctrl+K (Adding a Link) There isn't a button to create a hyperlink, despite the fact that there are keys to add animated GIFs, attachments, start a meeting, and alter the fonts in a chat. You can rapidly add a link to the text you are typing by using the keyboard shortcut Ctrl+K. You can write both the URL that the link points to and the display text. We frequently employ this by crafting phrases like "Please find the document to review here."

58

INTERACTION IN TEAMS

A set of communication tools provided by Microsoft Teams encourages team members to interact and work together. Team members are constantly on the go and frequently work from distant places apart from their teammates in the modern world. To increase productivity through collaboration and decision-making, it is imperative to have dependable virtual communication tools. We'll go over audio, video, images, chat, and other Microsoft Teams communication methods.

DISCUSSIONS

Discussions take place in team channels. They give team members a forum for topic discussion and message posting, to which all team members can respond. The decrease in email is one of the main advantages of chats. Unlike traditional email, conversations take place in a single location that all team members can see. Team members' visibility is restricted since email messages are kept in separate mail inboxes. Frequently, someone emails a group of individuals about a particular subject. The group context is therefore lost when that email is replied to without involving the entire group or sent to a specific person. As a result, team members are left out of the chain of emails and are not informed of important choices or debates pertaining to the subject. Preserving your organizational assets is one of the main benefits of using discussions. Team members can exchange crucial information and make decisions during discussions. The material stays in the channel for you and other viewers to access at a later time, even if every team member departs the company. A new member can catch up when they join the department, project, or organization. Because Microsoft Teams stores conversations, they can browse through them all in one location and rapidly catch up.

HOW TO INITIATE A DIALOGUE

- Select your preferred channel and navigate to the Conversations tab.
- Type your message in the text box at the bottom of the Conversations tab, then click the arrow in the text box's lower-right corner.

61

BRINGING UP A TEAM, CHANNEL, OR TEAM MEMBER

A list of names that begin with the few letters you type will appear for you to select from if you type the @ symbol after the name of a team member, channel, or team. A notification of the mention will be sent to the person you have selected. Everyone who favorited the channel gets a notification when you select one. If you select a team, a notification is sent to all team members. A team, channel, or team member might be informed in this fashion that they are the recipient of a message and should pay attention.

LIKING A MESSAGE

Clicking the "Like" button on someone's message is one way to show that you have read their discussion message or that you agree with them. This is comparable to Facebook's popular "Like" feature. You let the individual who posted the chat message know that you enjoyed it. By using the same button, you can reject a conversation.

HOW TO LIKE MESSAGES

- Move your mouse pointer over the message's right corner.
- To make it blue, click the thumbs-up icon

62

SAVING A MESSAGE FROM A CONVERSATION

Pressing the Save button on a message will save the conversation. Later, they might be seen in a central area.

To keep messages:

- Move your mouse pointer over the message's right corner.
- To make it pink, click the Save icon.

HOW TO SEE MESSAGES THAT HAVE BEEN SAVED

- In the Microsoft Teams app, click the icon for your picture in the lower-left corner.
- Click Saved.

Microsoft Teams' Chat feature allows for one-on-one or ad hoc group discussions with instant notification. If you have used Skype for Business, you are familiar with its chat feature. Chat offers real-time alerts. It is different from discussions in that team members will not be informed if they are not using that channel. Group chat is another feature that Microsoft Teams provides. You have the option of selecting either individuals or groups to whom you want to send a chat message. Information workers frequently ignore phone calls and other distractions in today's contemporary

63

workplaces since they reduce productivity. When you don't have a coworker's direct phone number, you can use the mobile app's chat feature to replace text messaging. Within the mobile application, team members can send a chat message, which will be received by the addressee. By allowing team members to have brief conversations and receive answers to queries whether they are in the office or on the go, chat enhances real-time collaboration and boosts productivity. By enabling teams to discuss project-related issues and tasks in real-time communication and swiftly reach decision points, group chat increases team productivity by cutting down on meetings and meeting duration.

HOW TO SEND A MESSAGE VIA CHAT

- In the Teams app, click the chat icon on the left.
- To the right of the search box, click the new chat paper-and-pencil icon.
- Type in the group or names you wish to mail.
- Click the arrow in the text box's lower right corner after typing your message there. You will notify everyone you sent the message to.

FORMATTING OPTIONS FOR CHAT MESSAGES

More possibilities for the conversation text are displayed when you expand the compose box. click the icon with the letter A and a paintbrush beneath the text box to enlarge the compose box. This will bring up the paragraph-formatting options, including headings and bullets, along with the tools to adjust the text's font, size, and color. Expanding the compose box also reveals the hyperlink addition option.

65

MAKING USE OF EMOJIS

Team members can communicate their feelings in chats and conversations by using emojis. Web 2.0 features featured on well-known social media platforms are provided by emojis. They give businesses a tool to add individuality to initiatives and provide more context. They use a variety of faces to convey your feelings to your teammates regarding a subject or message. You can use an ecstatic emoji to show your team members that you are thrilled about a project milestone that you have reached as the project manager. You might use a sad or humiliated emoji to convey that you missed a deadline.

Emojis allow personality-based communication to add more emotion to a project or task being managed in Microsoft Teams, which is useful in work-related situations like organizing a happy hour event or throwing a promotion party for a team member. If you're unsure of the meaning of a certain emoji, you can use the search box or move your cursor over it to find out. Emojis truly allow a person's personality to come through in their speech.

To include an emoji in a message from a chat or conversation:

- To add a new chat or discussion message, click the smiley face symbol beneath the text field.
- To locate an emotion, either use the search box or browse the emoji faces.

THE STICKERS

Editable pictures known as stickers can be included in chat and conversation messages. Many different sticker templates are included with Microsoft Teams. You may have a lot of

67

fun with your team by using stickers. Teams includes photos that you may alter with text to convey feelings through a picture and personalized statement. To include a sticker in a message from a chat or conversation:

- When creating a new chat or conversation message, click the square smiley sticker icon beneath the text field.
- Use the search box or scroll through the stickers.
- Click the Done button after entering any desired text.

GRAPHICS INTERCHANGE FORMAT, OR GIF

Graphics Interchange Format, or GIF for short, is a kind of file format that can hold animated pictures. Stickers and GIFs are similar, but the animation gives them more impact and excitement. However, unlike stickers, GIFs do not allow you to add text. Numerous GIFs are included in Microsoft Teams and can be used in chat and conversation messages. To include a GIF in a message for a chat or conversation:

- To add a new chat or conversation message, click the GIF symbol beneath the text field.
- Use the search box or scroll through the GIF.
- Select your preferred GIF.

68

LOOK UP PREVIOUS MESSAGES

From your channel chats or chat list, you can look up previous messages. Enter the name of the person who messaged you in the search bar, or use important terms from the message. Your search results can be filtered by the message's date, author, and subject.

VOICE CALLS

There are instances when communicating with a team member is necessary or when there is not enough time to type a chat message. In this case, voice calls are ideal. You will notice that the functionality is remarkably similar if you have ever used Skype for Business at work. Anyone in your company, even if they are not on any of your teams, can be voice called. You can also make calls to external phone numbers if your company has an Enterprise Voice license. To place a voice call:

- In the Microsoft Teams app, click the chat icon on the left.
- Use the search box to locate the person you wish to call, or choose them from your recent list. To make the call, you can follow the preceding instructions to create a new conversation.

69

- Click the phone symbol in the upper right corner of the chat message. The call screen will then appear.
- A notification that they are receiving a Teams call is sent to them via ringing. The call starts if they answer; if not, they are informed that the call was missed.

VIDEO CONVERSATIONS

Because you can see and hear the other person, video calling is the most intimate way to communicate in Teams. Each participant's face takes up the full screen during a Teams video conference, giving the impression that you are speaking with them in person. If you wish to send a link to a work product or are having problems hearing a team member during a video conversation, you can also send chat messages.

To place a video call:

- In the Teams app, click the chat icon on the left.
- Use the search box to locate the person you wish to video call, or choose them from your recent list. To make the video call, follow the preceding steps to create a new conversation.
- Click the video camera icon in the upper right corner of the chat message.

- The individual receives a ringing notification that they are receiving a Teams video call. The call starts if they answer; if not, they are informed that the call was missed.

SELECTING THE APPROPRIATE COMMUNICATION CHANNEL

A virtual workspace that handles a variety of office communication formats is Microsoft Teams. You can use chat to communicate with a team member one-on-one. The subjects covered in chat are comparable to those that would be covered in person when visiting a team member's workplace or bumping into them during a break. They typically respond quickly and are informal. The color circle in the lower right corner of each team member's profile image indicates whether they are available, away, or offline. Red indicates busy, yellow indicates away, green indicates available, and no color indicates offline. Similar to group chat, group chat is used for impromptu conversations with a team. One efficient method to cut down on the need for time-consuming formal meetings is to use group chats. Group chats allow you to easily communicate with several team members. To make it more intimate, you can also use audio and video calling to see and hear your teammates. You should use conversations if you want to post

71

a message that each team member can respond to at their own pace.

TEAM MEETINGS

Over the past few years, the corporate community has conducted a great deal of study and discussion around the time, money, and resources that are spent on meetings. Without taking up an hour or more of a team member's day to gather together, group chat and chats in Microsoft Teams provide useful ways to discuss issues and reach decisions. However, there are several circumstances where meetings are required. Microsoft Teams may be used to facilitate meetings for a variety of corporate purposes, including discussing status updates, reviewing project code, honing a sales strategy, and more.

Microsoft Teams offers three distinct meeting experiences: meet now, channel, and private. In addition to providing a variety of meeting experiences, Microsoft Teams offers a few distinct methods for scheduling and joining meetings. A pleasant and adaptable experience is made possible by a multitude of meeting features. There are several options for communication styles including video, phone chat, screen sharing, and in-meeting chat. The meeting choices in

72

Microsoft Teams, along with scheduling, joining, and participating.

PRIVATE CONSULTATIONS

The first kind of meeting we talk about is the most conventional since it looks like a commonly used Outlook meeting. Only team members who have been invited are permitted to attend private meetings. They might occur between two people or a large group of people. Either the Microsoft Teams app or an add-in for Outlook can be used to schedule meetings.

SETTING UP PRIVATE CONSULTATIONS

To use the Microsoft Teams app to set up a meeting:

- In the Microsoft Teams app, click the meetings icon on the left.
- Press the button to schedule a meeting.
- At the very least, complete the title, start and end dates, and times.
- Choose at least one person to invite in the Invite persons field. Choose them from the drop-down menu after starting to type their name in the designated field.
- Press the button to schedule a meeting.

73

Jason Taylor

CHAPTER FOUR

USING THE OUTLOOK ADD-IN TO SET UP A MEETING

To do this:

- Select the New Teams Meeting icon from the top ribbon in the Outlook calendar.
- Indicate the topic of the meeting as well as its start and end times.
- Press the Send icon.

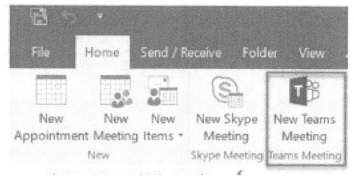

An email with a link to join the meeting in Teams will be sent to all invited participants. You may also click New Meeting and choose Teams Meeting when scheduling a Microsoft Teams meeting with the Outlook add-in. This is merely an alternative route to get the same goal while setting up your meeting.

HOW TO USE THE ASSISTANT FOR SCHEDULING

The scheduling assistant allows you to check when attendees are available or busy during the suggested meeting time.

- Select the Scheduling assistant link located beneath the finish time box to begin using it.
- Based on the attendees' availability, choose the meeting time.
- Depending on whether you are setting up a new meeting or amending an old one, click Schedule Meeting or Update.

BRINGING UNVERIFIED VISITORS TO MEETINGS

Teams gives you the ability to invite someone who is entirely outside of your company and might not even have the Microsoft Teams app loaded on their device to a private conference. To obtain information about the secret Microsoft Teams meeting and how to join it, an individual only has to have a working email account. When a guest clicks the link to join the meeting, they are asked to submit their name, though they can participate anonymously as well. Guests cannot share their screen if they do not have the Microsoft Teams app.

It is normal practice to hold virtual meetings with individuals who are not affiliated with an organization. When you need

76

to meet with a customer, stakeholder, contractor, vendor, or anybody else who does not have an Office 365 account with your company, this meeting capability comes in handy.

77

HOW TO PARTICIPATE IN PRIVATE SESSIONS

To participate in a meeting via the Teams app:

- The meetings icon on the Teams app's left side. The Agenda area displays any meetings you have scheduled in the future.

78

- Either click the Join button to the right of the meeting name or click the Join Microsoft Teams Meeting link in the meeting invite after selecting the meeting you want to join.

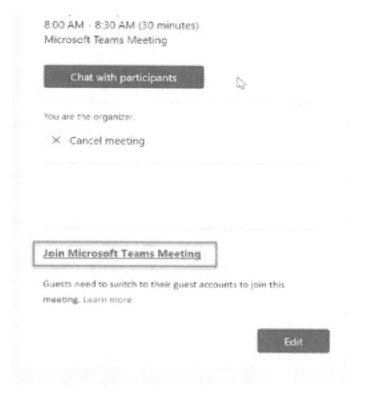

HOW TO JOIN A MEETING WITH THE OUTLOOK ADD-IN

- In the Outlook calendar, click the meeting to open the invite.

79

- Click Join Microsoft Teams Meeting.

CHANNEL MEETINGS

Channel meetings are scheduled meetings that occur in a team's channel, based on the topic. Channel meetings have several benefits. One benefit is that they make it easy to swiftly invite everyone from a team to a meeting. Another benefit is that information about the meeting is preserved in the channel as an organizational asset. While working in Teams, it is evident to team members that a meeting is underway on a channel: a camera icon appears to the right of the channel name. In the channel chats, a huge notice is posted as the meeting starts. The message shows each person who has joined the meeting by displaying their profile photographs in a little circle at the upper right of the message. At the bottom of the meeting message, you notice the chat. Additionally, a timer tells how long the meeting has been taking place.

SETTING UP MEETINGS FOR CHANNELS

The Microsoft Teams app is the sole way to book channel meetings; the Outlook add-in is not an option. When a channel meeting is planned, an email notification is sent to every team member.

80

Take note: The duration of the meeting, the participants, and the talk are automatically saved in the channel when the meeting is over.

HOW TO ARRANGE A MEETING VIA THE CHANNEL

- In the Microsoft Teams app, select the meetings icon on the left.
- Press the button to schedule a meeting.
- At the very least, complete the title, start and end dates, and times.
- Choose a channel from the drop-down menu labeled "Select a channel to meet."
- Press the button to schedule a meeting.

PARTICIPATING IN AN AUDIO CONFERENCE MEETING

When on the go, Microsoft Teams participants can join meetings by phone. When someone attending a meeting doesn't have internet connection, this is helpful. Dial-in instructions are included in the Teams meeting invite for participants who have this feature.

Note: Dial-in instructions are only sent to meeting attendees who have Office 365's audio conferencing functionality enabled.

AGENDA FOR THE MEETING

You can view all of the forthcoming private and channel meetings to which you have been invited in one place on the meeting agenda. You view every meeting for the week by default. You can switch the view to only display meetings for the day by clicking the blocked icon in the agenda's upper-right corner.

MEET NOW MEETINGS

All team members can meet impromptu during Meet Now meetings. A team can be brought together in an emergency or a message can be swiftly shared with others via Meet Now meetings. In that they are started and occur inside a channel, they are comparable to channel meetings. A conversation message that looks the same as it does for channel meetings is added to the channel when a Meet Now meeting begins. The Meet Now meeting conversation messages include the meeting name, participants, amount of time that has passed, and chat messages. A meeting is in progress, as indicated by the camera icon to the right of the channel name and the names of the team members. Meet Now meetings differ in

82

that the person who starts the meeting has the option to record the meeting.

HOW TO BEGIN A MEET NOW SESSION

- In the conversations tab of the channel where you wish to have the meeting, click the camera icon beneath the text box.

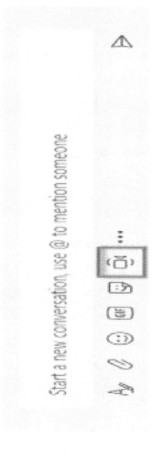

83

- Click the "Meet now" button after entering a topic.

PARTICIPANTS' MEETING CONTROLS

In Microsoft Teams meetings, participants are in charge of their participation style and the information they exchange. It is advised to use voice and video in meetings to maximize their effectiveness. Participants, however, have the option of using voice or appearing in a video. Additionally, participants have the option to share their screen. If you don't want people to see your email or anything else private, Microsoft Teams provides a feature that lets you select which window on your desktop you want to share. The participant controls are located in the center of the meeting screen. It is not until you move your mouse into that broad area that you can see the controls.

TURNING OFF THE MICROPHONE

Everyone in the meeting may become highly distracted if someone is using their microphone while there is background noise. Unless you are speaking, it is excellent practice to keep the microphone muted. You might have forgotten to unmute yourself, so check your microphone if you are speaking and nobody is answering!

84

HOW TO TURN OFF THE MICROPHONE

- Point the mouse pointer to the center of the conference screen.
- Press the icon for the microphone.

Use the same methods to unmute. When the microphone symbol is muted, a slash passes through it.

TURNING OFF VIDEO

Video is the most effective way to communicate with other meeting attendees. People are more likely to comprehend your message when they can see your facial expressions in addition to hearing you speak. Video can be simply turned off for situations where you don't want people to see you, including when you're multitasking or not in a formal meeting setting.

HOW TO TURN OFF THE VIDEO

- Position the mouse pointer in the center of the meeting screen.
- Click the video camera icon.

Use the same instructions to restart the video. Your profile picture will appear when you speak (instead of video) if you have one.

SHARING SCREENS

One very useful feature is screen sharing. Screen sharing is frequently used to demonstrate presentation slides or to guide participants through a procedure or work tool. Except for guests who are not authorized and are not using the Microsoft Teams app, all participants are able to share their screen.

HOW TO SHARE A SCREEN

- Position the mouse pointer in the center of the meeting screen.
- Click the icon for the computer screen.
- Decide if you wish to share an app or your desktop. Click the desired app or screen.
- Click the computer screen icon once more to terminate screen sharing.

HOW TO TAKE OVER THE SCREEN

It could be necessary for another participant to take over a meeting member's screen while they are sharing it in order to illustrate anything. A participant has the ability to both grant and request control over their screen.

TO TAKE CONTROL THE SCREEN

- When screen sharing, select the Give control drop-down menu in the upper center of the screen.

86

- Select the person's name that you wish to provide control to.

MULTITASKING IN TEAMS

Participating in a meeting and working within the app is made possible by Microsoft Teams. The meeting will shrink to a little window on the upper left corner of the Microsoft Teams application if you just click out of it anywhere in the program. Click the mini meeting window to get back to the meeting in a full window.

ENDING A MEETING

To end a meeting:

- Position the mouse pointer in the center of the meeting screen.
- Click the red phone symbol.

MEETING REGULATIONS FOR COORDINATORS

In order to ensure that the meeting goes successfully, meeting organizers have controls in place. The meeting's organizers have the authority to remove attendees, mute attendees, and admit attendees from the lobby.

ACCEPTING ATTENDEES FROM THE LOBBY

Admitting verified attendees who entered the meeting through the lobby is one of the responsibilities of the meeting

87

organizer. The names of the people waiting in the lobby may need to be carefully reviewed, depending on the topic of the discussion. You don't want someone who shouldn't be there to enter a meeting where sensitive topics are being discussed.

HOW TO ALLOW SOMEONE TO ENTER FROM THE LOBBY

- Click the checkmark next to the visitor's name.
- Rejecting someone from the meeting is done by clicking the X to the right of their name.

PARTICIPANTS WHO MUTE

Sometimes a participant may have moved away from their desk or fail to notice that their microphone is open. The organizer has the option to mute attendees if background noise or someone talking outside of the meeting is interfering with the meeting. Since the meeting lets you know who is speaking at the moment, you will be able to tell who is creating the noise. Additionally, you can choose to mute every participant. When there are a lot of people attending a meeting, this feature is extremely helpful.

HOW TO SILENCE AN INDIVIDUAL

- In the list of attendees for the meeting, click the ellipse (...) to the right of the participant's name.
- Select "Mute Participant."

88

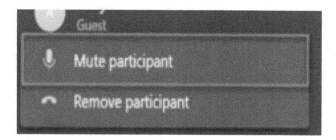

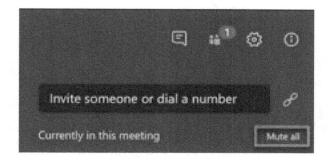

The present distraction has been resolved, but the participant will be able to unmute their microphone whenever they wish to talk again.

Take note: Click the Mute everyone link above the list of attendees to mute everyone in the meeting.

89

REMOVING PARTICIPANTS

Sometimes a participant is invited by mistake or is too disruptive. The meeting organizer has the authority to kick someone out under certain circumstances.

HOW TO SILENCE AN INDIVIDUAL

- In the list of attendees for the meeting, click the ellipse (...) to the right of the participant's name.
- Click Remove participant.

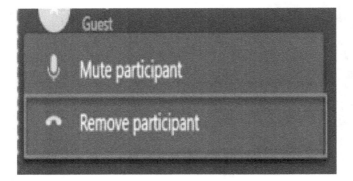

90

CHAPTER FIVE

ADOPTION OF USERS IN TEAMS

Have you ever received a memo informing you and your teammates about a new intranet that they must utilize, and heard the groaning and watched the eyes roll? Has it irritated you when leadership has informed you that the system and procedure for performance reviews are changing for the third time in two years? Information technology executives will likely cite user acceptance as the most difficult aspect of deploying new applications.

User adoption is the process by which employees of a company embrace and fully utilize newly provided software or tools in their workplace. For several reasons, organizations find this difficult. Once they get into a routine, people just do not like to break it, even if it will save them time and make their lives easier later on. This is particularly true when they are under a lot of stress or have a lot of work to do. Switching gears and using a new software or product can be challenging when individuals of the organization are having trouble meeting deadlines or have competing priorities.

Furthermore, new software and technologies are frequently not trusted. End users lose interest in new software if a

91

business has experienced unsuccessful software rollouts in the past. This is particularly true if a large number of individuals lose their jobs and/or time, or if this is how it is seen. Another factor that may hinder user adoption is training. Members of well-meaning organizations may attempt to use a new tool or piece of software but find it difficult to use effectively. They are likely to turn to outdated tools or look for workarounds that don't require the new program if they are unable to promptly fix it.

Don't take short cuts since user adoption planning is just as crucial as implementation planning. If user acceptance is poor, it won't matter how well Microsoft Teams is technically implemented. Numerous IT specialists have observed these problems with user adoption afflict their rollouts of collaboration software for many years. Organizations can use the numerous lessons learnt to make sure that Microsoft Teams user adoption is successful.

WHAT TO USE AND WHEN TO USE IT FOR COLLABORATION

Yammer is an Office 365 solution for information sharing and social networking throughout the entire company. Office 365 Groups is another of Microsoft's more recent offerings. Members of a group can work together and complete tasks

92

using the Outlook client in Office 365 Groups, which offer a shared workspace with email, conversations, files, and events. Though they are somewhat related in the background, it is crucial to note that Microsoft Teams is a platform with even more functionality.

The benefits of using Microsoft Teams are numerous. Even if a team may consist of up to 2,500 people, we do not advise using Microsoft Teams only for information and announcements at the organizational level. An organization's intranet should not be replaced by Microsoft Teams. It can be a little confusing at times to know which tool to use when.

USE OF CASES IN THE REAL WORLD

Examples of how to make the most of Microsoft Teams' features include the following. Every business is unique, therefore it's critical to keep in mind that Microsoft Teams can be incorporated into the IT strategy in a number of ways.

Use Case 1: Organizing a Novel Project

In underprivileged schools, a group is launching a new program to teach kids about eating well. It adds all of the people working on the project as team members and forms a private team. For each of the four schools the project is aimed at, a new channel is added. The team members talk about their lesson ideas, material development, scheduling,

93

and other school-related subjects in those channels. They store the personalized learning resources and forms they made for every school under the documents tab in these channels. Each school's designated team members have a favorite and subscribe to the channel for that school to ensure they are informed about all channel operations. Discussions about issues related to the entire project, like funding and teamwork, take place on the General channel tasks. A Power BI chart with metrics on the number of kids from each school who have taken part in the project is displayed on a tab that has been set up. The procedures that team members should adhere to upon arriving at a school are described in the wiki. Group chat messages are frequently used by team members to swiftly agree on planning choices.

Use Case 2: Cooperation Across Departments

The IT department of a mid-sized business has a dedicated team for the HR department. The department's many operations, including hiring, benefits, payroll, and training, have their own channels. The benefits service, which the entire team frequently utilizes during the workday, has its own tab on the General channel. The recruitment channel includes tabs for a Microsoft Word document that is frequently consulted for advice when cold phoning potential

94

hires and a SharePoint list that houses recruitment prospects. The main purpose of the training channel is to talk about the training materials that are being created.

Team members utilize a tab that holds a Microsoft Excel document that the company uses to keep track of the required training for its personnel. Numerous documents from benefits vendors that are given to employees are kept in the benefits channel.

The discussions tab is highly busy during the time of year when people are shopping for benefits plans. To talk about any new developments and problems, the team meets once a week in the benefits channel. Team members are actively using the payroll channel to resolve time card inconsistencies and ask each other questions regarding their payroll software.

Use Case 3: IT Project Management

The 50 employees of a small IT consulting firm are dispersed across multiple nations and all work from home. They offer IT support and solutions to five sizable, long-term clientele. Because they don't want employees to see the content of a client they aren't working with, Microsoft Teams has a distinct team for every client.

95

Every team has channels for testing, development, and project management. The Planner app is displayed by project managers via a tab in the project management channel in Office 365, where tasks are assigned and monitored. Additionally, they use Microsoft Teams to plan daily stand-up meetings, monitor attendance, and request updates via the meeting chat.

The members of the quality assurance team use the testing channels. They talk about testing procedures and timetables. Additionally, they have a tab to a quality log in a SharePoint list. The development channels feature tabs that show Visual Studio Team Services, a tool that developers use to monitor problems and store code. They frequently conduct code reviews and screen sharing during sessions.

Pilots

Because of its great adaptability, Microsoft Teams may be used to suit a wide range of corporate requirements for meetings, chat, and collaboration. With so many customizable features and settings, Microsoft Teams may be utilized in a wide variety of ways. As a result, it is advised to start with a small-scale Teams rollout. By offering a means of fine-tuning the nuances of your company culture without affecting the entire organization, a Teams pilot reduces risk.

96

The advantages of conducting a pilot are as follows:

- Identifies the areas in which users encounter difficulties so that training can be most effective.
- Examines trends in the pilot group's Microsoft Teams usage.
- Gathers input from the pilot group and transforms it into practical suggestions to enhance the company's Microsoft Teams experience.
- Inspires a group of people to support and advocate for Microsoft Teams in the future.
- Identifies any security or performance problems
- Fixes any technical problems that impact user experience, like firewall configuration, application incompatibility, or authentication annoyances.

In order to significantly improve the likelihood of effective user adoption, pick one or a small number of projects, departments, or initiatives to use Microsoft Teams and offer input before it is made public. It's crucial to choose the appropriate group of candidates for a pilot position.

In general, the most crucial traits for a pilot group are a good mix of skill levels and positive attitudes. Because IT workers are typically more educated about Microsoft Teams and skilled at integrating new software, using the IT department

97

for your trial group may not be representative of how the rest of the firm would use the platform. Additionally, you don't want to pick a group that is too busy to offer comments or make the most of Microsoft Teams.

The degree of structure required for the pilot depends on the organization's size, culture, and technological capabilities. The pilot group will have the abilities necessary to maximize the pilot's performance if they receive some kind of training prior to their start. At the very least, a pilot start meeting that describes the pilot's Objectives, Anticipations, Timetable, Criteria for success.

TIPS FOR USER ADOPTION

Adoption by users is both a science and an art. The most crucial thing is to have a plan, but also to be adaptable enough to change course if necessary. When implementing Microsoft Teams, your company might already have knowledge on user adoption from earlier software rollouts. These pointers are an excellent place to start.

DESCRIBE YOUR GOALS

Choosing to use Microsoft Teams for the proper purposes is the first step towards a successful implementation. A group of people working on a project or job function that requires them to communicate, work together, and hold meetings is

98

the main target business scenario for implementing Microsoft Teams.

Additionally, it is a good idea to determine the purpose of your Microsoft Teams rollout before implementing it. Even though Microsoft Teams is a brand-new and exciting program, implementing it just because everyone else is using it or because it's new isn't always the best course of action. Adoption is aided by knowing the difficulties your users face at work and how Microsoft Teams may help them overcome those difficulties.

Microsoft Teams can tackle these issues in a number of ways, including the following:

- Creates the impression that distant workers are in the same office, strengthening their sense of connection.
- Saves time by eliminating the need to launch numerous apps in order to work with coworkers.
- By keeping related artifacts in one place, it makes them easier to find.

Although the motivations of every business vary, spending some time figuring them out will help you lay the groundwork for a Microsoft Teams deployment that works.

99

EXPLAIN THE ADVANTAGES

Launch a communications campaign emphasizing the advantages for users months before Microsoft Teams is made available to the public in an organization. Some companies have employees whose primary responsibility is to create and implement communication plans. For other organizations, posting an announcement on the intranet or bringing up Microsoft Teams during meetings is adequate.

CHOOSE THE APPROPRIATE TEAM OWNERS

Having team owners who support Microsoft Teams is essential. Anyone with prior ownership experience or a particular interest in another collaborative technology, like SharePoint, would be a good fit. Team owners engage with team members, and it is crucial that the owners have a pleasant attitude and complete awareness of how Microsoft Teams operates. Team owners should feel empowered to make decisions and try new ways to use Microsoft Teams to maximize the benefits. Forcing someone who is too busy to be a team owner, or who is uninterested in being a team owner, is detrimental to user adoption.

100

METHODS FOR TEAM OWNERS TO INVOLVE THEIR MEMBERS

Setting a great example on how to use Microsoft Teams is the best method for team owners to keep their team members interested. When team owners see a long group email exchange, they should answer, "Let's take this conversation to Microsoft Teams." Often, team members advise scheduling a meeting to address something that could be handled in conversations in Microsoft Teams. Team owners can start a conversation in Microsoft Teams and let team members know that time could be saved if the matter is discussed there.

If a team member is sluggish to start using Microsoft Teams, the team owner can @mention the individual in conversations so that they receive notifications and are engaged in the collaborative efforts. Being accessible to respond to inquiries is another excellent way team owners may assist their members. Team members are considerably more likely to use Microsoft Teams if they have someone to reach out to when they are confused or have questions.

PUT AN END TO DUPLICATION

When consumers feel they must complete a task twice, it is a huge turn-off for them. When some users adopt Microsoft

101

Teams and others haven't, this can occur. An illustration would be if someone uploaded a document to a Microsoft Teams channel and messaged a team member to request that they evaluate it. The team member never views the message since they haven't embraced Microsoft Teams. The user then ends up having to email them the paper and ask them again to evaluate it. This will inevitably occur in the initial phases of a Microsoft Teams release; however, it must be fixed or there will be much frustration. It might require leadership to convey that everyone is expected to use Microsoft Teams and read their messages.

CONSULT WITH USERS

It is a mistake to deploy Microsoft Teams to a company without regularly interacting with people to get their feedback and address any queries. This acts as a reminder to utilize it and gives people a sense of support. As long as steps are taken to enhance user experiences in response to feedback, checking in with users can help increase user adoption. Too frequently, consumers encounter problems but choose not to report them because no one asks.

ALLOW THE USERS TO ENJOY THEIR TIME

Microsoft Teams' GIFs, stickers, and emojis undoubtedly add a playful element that most users find enjoyable. This

102

can help create an environment where team members feel free to express themselves. Leave the GIFs and stickers alone unless there is a good reason to limit or disable them. In the event that the stickers and GIFs are misused or overdone,

Only a small percentage of consumers might require assistance. If the problem is widespread, inform all users of the solution and, if required, change the settings. A crucial component of user adoption is training. Although Microsoft Teams is really easy to use, even the most technologically advanced companies need have some instruction and direction. Training should ideally start as soon as Microsoft Teams is implemented within the company. Training materials must to be accessible to users as well. Users must have an easy way to get their questions answered. One suggestion is to create a team channel with training materials and a conversations page where team members can respond to inquiries.

The following ideas should be understood by all users:

- How to use Microsoft Teams;
- How to schedule and attend meetings;
- How to use teams and channels;
- What tabs and connectors are;

- How to chat and participate in conversations;
- How to share and access files;
- How to manage notifications

Team owners must receive training on extra responsibilities in Microsoft Teams. Team owners should ideally also be accessible to respond to inquiries from team members. Team owners should be aware of the distinctions between their capabilities in Microsoft Teams and those of a team member.

The following ideas should be understood by team owners:

- How to add team members to a team;
- How to manage team settings;
- How to create, edit, and remove a team

There are several different training films available in Microsoft Teams. Microsoft understood how crucial it was to properly instruct users on how to utilize a program. These films may not contain all the information you need to make available to your consumers, despite the fact that they are incredibly beneficial and a significant upgrade over some previously published applications. You could include any specialized training you believe your users need before they can use the team in this procedure.

104

CONTINUOUS OBSERVATION AND ENHANCEMENT

Not everyone considers adoption to be a continuous process. Regretfully, a lot of firms believe they lack the necessary resources or are unaware of the consequences of not implementing continuous adoption. As with any software, the more you use it, the more you'll discover methods to make your interactions with it better. You can discover that the software is no longer used after a while. Almost invariably, this happens for valid reasons. It is important that someone is responsible for addressing the issue and resolving it to ensure long-term success with the application.

Microsoft understands the requirement for continued monitoring as part of the overall adoption of Teams. Microsoft introduced use reports in the Office 365 admin area for most of its products. To view these reports, you need to have your Office 365 administrator assemble them for you or give you an admin position in the Office 365 admin center to allow you to build these reports yourself.

Currently, Microsoft Teams allows for the processing of two distinct reports:

- Activity related to Microsoft Teams usage
- Use of Microsoft Teams devices

105

The Activity and Users tabs in the usage activity report display data in a graph. Additionally, there is comprehensive data on how many channel messages, chats, calls, and meetings each user has participated in, as well as when they were last active in a team. You can draw several conclusions from this data about what might be going on if long-term user adoption begins to decline.

The benefit of these reports is that you can easily identify which users may have been extremely active before their activity abruptly decreased because they list each user's activity. You know who users to contact first if there is an issue with prolonged use. The Microsoft Teams Device Usage report is available to you or your Office 365 administrator. This report's ability to show you how many people utilize mobile devices to access Microsoft Teams is one advantage. Additionally, you can look into the problem if the statistics for a particular mobile device suddenly start to decline. We noted earlier in the book that mobile devices lack some of the features seen in web and client interfaces. The mobile app might have caused a problem for customers that you are unaware of if you notice a declining trend in a certain mobile operating system (not because it is going extinct, like with Palm).

106

Hopefully, the most important lesson learned from this chapter is that implementing Microsoft Teams successfully and successfully over the long run in your company is not something you should ignore or assume will only take a short while. Although putting all of these tactics and concepts into practice or finding stakeholders to take ownership of them may not be simple, at least you will be aware that your chances of success will be far lower than those of those who have. We go over how to manage Microsoft Teams in your company in the upcoming chapter. Governance and user adoption go hand in hand because without governance, your Microsoft Teams deployment will operate poorly and lose functionality, which will eventually drive away users.

LEADERSHIP

User adoption and governance go hand in one. A carefully considered governance plan guarantees that Microsoft Teams is utilized and maintained as intended. If Microsoft Teams is user-friendly and well-managed, users will embrace it. A strong governance plan guarantees that the organization's assets are appropriately stored and utilized, as well as that the user experience stays good. Microsoft Teams' primary selling point is that it facilitates faster and easier collaboration by giving team members a single place to communicate, exchange material, and have meetings.

107

But only if you take the time to design the management and administration of the service before launching it for your users will the benefits become apparent. There are risks that will outweigh these advantages in the absence of a governance framework.

You may create a governance strategy that guarantees the security of content and the ease of use of Microsoft Teams, which will increase user adoption, with the use of real-world examples and explanations.

MAKING YOUR OWN STRATEGY

The following should be included at the very least when creating your own governance plan for Microsoft Teams:

- How to set up your team's structure (this may vary depending on the team you form)
- How to make it possible for individuals to seek or form a new team (a procedure for creating teams)
- How to decide whether a new team has to be formed

To help you develop your own governance plan, let's now go over each bullet point in greater depth.

STRUCTURE OF ORGANIZATION FOR CHANNELS AND TEAMS

If Microsoft Teams is implemented with default settings and users are not given any instruction, it might quickly become unmanageable. All users have the ability to create new channels and teams by default. The structure of SharePoint is one analogy that many IT experts might use. Many users were allowed to construct new sites at their own discretion prior to the recognition of the significance of governance. An unmanageable environment swiftly developed in the absence of adequate training, planning, and strategic thinking regarding the timing of the creation of new sites. Let's apply the lessons learnt to prevent this from happening with Microsoft Teams, since the absence of governance hurt user adoption of SharePoint.

To plan how to set up teams and channels, it is crucial to examine the work functions, departments, products, initiatives, and/or projects of your company. The ability to define permissions just at the team level is an important thing to keep in mind. All content in channels is open and accessible to every team member associated with the channel until Microsoft develops secure channels.

109

AdviceIt is crucial to think about who should have access to what content while planning the channels and teams' organizational structures.

An example of an organizational structure is shown below where each main department has a team, and each office that is part of the department has a channel.

110

A crucial component of user adoption is training. Although Microsoft Teams is really easy to use, even the most technologically advanced companies need have some instruction and direction. Training should ideally start as soon as Microsoft Teams is implemented within the company. Training materials must to be accessible to users as well. Users must have an easy way to get their questions answered. One suggestion is to create a team channel with training materials and a conversations page where team members can respond to inquiries.

The following ideas should be understood by all users:

- How to use Microsoft Teams;
- How to schedule and attend meetings;
- How to use teams and channels;
- What tabs and connectors are;
- How to chat and participate in conversations;
- How to share and access files;
- How to manage notifications

Team owners must receive training on extra responsibilities in Microsoft Teams. Team owners should ideally also be accessible to respond to inquiries from team members. Team owners should be aware of the distinctions between their

111

capabilities in Microsoft Teams and those of a team member. The following ideas should be understood by team owners:

- How to add team members to a team;
- How to manage team settings;
- How to create, edit, and remove a team

There are several different training films available in Microsoft Teams. Microsoft understood how crucial it was to properly instruct users on how to utilize a program. These films may not contain all the information you need to make available to your consumers, despite the fact that they are incredibly beneficial and a significant upgrade over some previously published applications. Developing a procedure for users to request a team is a far better idea than letting anyone create a team whenever they want. You could include any specialized training you believe your users need before they can use the team in this procedure.

CONTINUOUS OBSERVATION AND ENHANCEMENT

Not everyone considers adoption to be a continuous process. Regretfully, a lot of firms believe they lack the necessary resources or are unaware of the consequences of not implementing continuous adoption. As with any software, the more you use it, the more you'll discover methods to make your interactions with it better. You can discover that the software is no longer used after a while. Almost invariably, this happens for valid reasons. It is important that someone is responsible for addressing the issue and resolving it to ensure long-term success with the application. Microsoft understands the requirement for continued monitoring as part of the overall adoption of Teams. Microsoft introduced use reports in the Office 365 admin area for most of its products. To view these reports, you need to have your Office 365 administrator assemble them for you or give you an admin position in the Office 365 admin center to allow you to build these reports yourself. Currently, Microsoft Teams allows for the processing of two distinct reports:

- Activity related to Microsoft Teams usage
- Use of Microsoft Teams devices

The Activity and Users tabs in the usage activity report display data in a graph. Additionally, there is comprehensive data on how many channel messages, chats, calls, and meetings each user has participated in, as well as when they were last active in a team. You can draw several conclusions from this data about what might be going on if long-term user adoption begins to decline. The benefit of these reports

113

is that you can easily identify which users may have been extremely active before their activity abruptly decreased because they list each user's activity. You know who users to contact first if there is an issue with prolonged use. The Microsoft Teams Device Usage report is available to you or your Office 365 administrator. This report's ability to show you how many people utilize mobile devices to access Microsoft Teams is one advantage. Additionally, you can look into the problem if the statistics for a particular mobile device suddenly start to decline. We noted earlier in the book that mobile devices lack some of the features seen in web and client interfaces. The mobile app might have caused a problem for customers that you are unaware of if you notice a declining trend in a certain mobile operating system (not because it is going extinct, like with Palm).

CHAPTER SIX
LEADERSHIP

User adoption and governance go hand in one. A carefully considered governance plan guarantees that Microsoft Teams is utilized and maintained as intended. If Microsoft Teams is user-friendly and well-managed, users will embrace it. A strong governance plan guarantees that the organization's assets are appropriately stored and utilized, as well as that the user experience stays good. Microsoft Teams' primary selling point is that it facilitates faster and easier collaboration by giving team members a single place to communicate, exchange material, and have meetings. But only if you take the time to design the management and administration of the service before launching it for your users will the benefits become apparent. There are risks that will outweigh these advantages in the absence of a governance framework.

You may create a governance strategy that guarantees the security of content and the ease of use of Microsoft Teams, which will increase user adoption, with the use of real-world examples and explanations.

115

MAKING YOUR OWN STRATEGY

The following should be included at the very least when creating your own governance plan for Microsoft Teams:

- How to set up your team's structure (this may vary depending on the team you form)
- How to make it possible for individuals to seek or form a new team (a procedure for creating teams)
- How to decide whether a new team has to be formed

Knowing how to archive outdated or underutilized teams; being aware of features and organizational settings. To help you develop your own governance plan, let's now go over each bullet point in greater depth.

STRUCTURE OF ORGANIZATION FOR CHANNELS AND TEAMS

If Microsoft Teams is implemented with default settings and users are not given any instruction, it might quickly become unmanageable. All users have the ability to create new channels and teams by default. The structure of SharePoint is one analogy that many IT experts might use. Many users were allowed to construct new sites at their own discretion prior to the recognition of the significance of governance. An unmanageable environment swiftly developed in the absence of adequate training, planning, and strategic thinking regarding the timing of the creation of new sites. Let's apply the lessons learnt to prevent this from happening with Microsoft Teams, since the absence of governance hurt user adoption of SharePoint. To plan how to set up teams and channels, it is crucial to examine the work functions, departments, products, initiatives, and/or projects of your company. The ability to define permissions just at the team level is an important thing to keep in mind. All content in channels is open and accessible to every team member associated with the channel until Microsoft develops secure channels.

Advice: It is crucial to think about who should have access to what content while planning the channels and teams' organizational structures. The next section explains many of the concepts you may utilize as a process because there are so many ways a company could implement a Teams formation process. There is no secret formula for choosing a procedure. You can choose between the two options by weighing the advantages and disadvantages of each and comparing them to the requirements of your company.

OPTIONS FOR CREATING TEAMS

We outline the possibilities in this section along with their benefits and drawbacks.

117

New item

Content Type

Item

Proposed Team Name

Enter text here

Requestor

Enter a name or email address

Department

Enter text here

Purpose of New Team

Enter text here

Team Owners

Enter a name or email address

Private or Public?

Private

External Users?

Enter text here

Attachments

Add attachments

Save   Cancel

118

ABSENCE OF A TEAM FORMATION PROCEDURE

For most firms, just "flipping the switch" to activate Microsoft Teams without any preparation or thought is not an option. We do not recommend using this method unless you are completely unconcerned about the data. Taking note of this, the benefits and drawbacks are listed below. Advantages of this strategy include the highest potential for short-term acceptance, little preparation and training needs, and the quickest implementation time.

DRAWBACKS

In the event that you need to manage, organize, sort, or reuse your data over time, the negative effects of this procedure are significant. Many of the potential drawbacks of the approach are described later in this chapter.

TEAM REQUEST EXAMINED BY THE HELP DESK OR ADMIN

Implementing a team request procedure that creates a SharePoint list for users to submit is one example of a team creation process. After reviewing the requests, an administrator, help desk, or IT teams specialist forms the team if the request is accepted.

Advantages of this solution include its speedy implementation and the fact that the company incurs no extra

119

expenses. It may be possible to stop users from submitting duplicate team names by configuring the SharePoint list.

DRAWBACKS

Each request must be processed by a human, which consumes time and money. Additionally, it necessitates that you disable user group creation and restrict who can establish new teams and groups.

PUTTING REQUESTORS IN A SECURITY GROUP FOR TEAMS

Microsoft has also suggested this strategy. It may be regarded as a "meet us in the middle" concept. To put it into practice, your Office 365 administrator must form a security group and add only people you want and trust. Before adding people to this group, you could make sure they've finished their training.

Advantages

This method has the advantage of allowing trustworthy users to form teams on their own, which frees up time for your help desk or IT administrators. Additionally, it enables those users to build other Office 365 apps like Planners, Yammer groups, and Office 365 groups without requiring additional communication from others.

120

Drawbacks

Putting someone in the security group does not ensure that they will abide by all of your regulations. Users might not follow the guidelines if you have naming conventions, wish to avoid duplicate names, or want to limit the number of teams formed because of organizational and space constraints.

REQUEST LIST IN SHAREPOINT THAT STARTS A FLOW

This approach is the least programmatic technique to achieve the goal of totally preventing users from building teams (and any other applications connected to groups). It entails creating a SharePoint list and programming it to run any necessary checks before the user submits the list item. When a list item is submitted, a flow is started that creates a team via the REST API and notifies your users of its creation.

Advantages

The benefits of this strategy include regulating the quantity, nomenclature, and occurrence of new teams. Additionally, compared to the next final proposal, it requires a little less

121

programming. Your users won't have to wait for the new team to be formed because it is nearly instantaneous.

Drawbacks

This method's drawbacks are that it requires someone with some technical expertise and takes time to construct. Additionally, it needs approval from your organization to be used, and if you have run a lot of requests, it may result in extra expenses. Last but not least, you won't be able to modify the elements that make up a team if you need to (for example, by changing the SharePoint site collection to prevent external sharing). Additionally, users are restricted from requesting any group-based applications.

SHAREPOINT REQUEST LIST USING CODE OR POWERSHELL

Of all the concepts we have covered, this one is the most complex. This strategy will work best for you, though, if you work for a really strict company that requires structure, governance, and control. After a user requests a team from a SharePoint list, the list elements are processed by a scheduled job on a Windows server or Azure Functions, which subsequently notifies the requestor and creates the team.

122

Advantages

The benefit of this approach is that it has complete control over your staff. Within the constraints that Microsoft permits, you might alter the appearance of your team or add certain individuals to it. Additionally, you could change associated components like the sharing settings for SharePoint site collections. It can also be used to establish a yearly review process or to keep track of other team information.

Drawbacks

The drawback of this strategy is that it necessitates the creation of a proficient coder. To run the code, you also need a Windows server or an Azure account. Your users will have to wait before they can use the team if you decide to schedule the code. Users are also subject to the need that they request any group-based application.

If all of these concepts seem too complicated and time-consuming, you can go online for a third-party program that does everything automatically. These items typically have high prices and should be carefully considered before being bought.

123

ASSESSING THE NEED TO FORM A NEW TEAM

There are a few things to think about while evaluating a request for a new team in order to decide whether or not the team should be formed. First and foremost, you want to make sure that you don't create a team that already exists in order to avoid duplication. Additionally, you should refrain from forming too many teams. For end users, duplication causes confusion and frustration. Users that have to transfer between teams during the day to complete their task and receive an excessive number of notifications find it annoying when there are several teams.

A new team will be required if external guest users to be included on the team. The rationale for this is that outside of the work they are doing, outsider guests usually cannot access any team content. If external guests should not be able to access the other team channels, a new team must be formed, even if the proposed new team is a channel under an existing team.

Consider the following questions while determining whether to form a new team:

- Does the same department, initiative, project, case, or account already have a team or channel.

124

- Is there already a team with the same members as the one being suggested?
- Will there be outside guest team members present?

FUNCTIONS AND ACCOUNTABILITIES

Roles and duties must be assigned, just like in any system or process. It is necessary to assign and communicate primary roles in teams in order to ensure accountability. These positions include team owner, team member, Office 365 administrator, and decision maker.

MAKER OF DECISIONS

There are decisions about Teams that must be made continuously. This covers choices for setup, implementation, integration with other apps, and team and channel creation procedures. The decision maker may be in charge of deciding whether or not a team should be formed if an organization chooses to restrict who is able to form teams. In order to give technical leadership and make choices about the use and upkeep of collaborative platforms, many large organizations have established governance boards. Because they take too long to make decisions and micromanage SharePoint to the point where it is worthless, we have seen SharePoint governance boards destroy user adoption and cooperation.

125

User adoption suffers when IT and leadership personnel, who typically serve on these boards, are either too busy or don't want to participate. In certain instances, corporate policies necessitate the establishment of an official governance board, or the governance board model works well for making decisions regarding other collaborative technologies.

Designating experts to promote and speed up collaboration and act as the point of contact for Office 365 administrators, team owners, and end users is an additional choice for decision-making. These collaboration experts ought to be well-versed in Teams and any additional collaboration platforms the company use. A cooperation specialist guarantees that inquiries and requests are addressed in a timely manner.

ADMINISTRATOR FOR OFFICE 365

Microsoft Teams tenant-wide options are accessible to Office 365 administrators. They are responsible for offering support and direction in technical administration. Any performance-related problems encountered when utilizing Microsoft Teams are also their responsibility.

OWNER OF THE TEAM

The crucial duty of team leadership falls on team owners. Owners of the team keep an eye on the content to ensure that it is appropriate and useful. Additionally, team owners have a number of parameters that they can modify for the team, which has a direct effect on how team members interact with one another. Up to 10 team owners are permitted per team in Teams. Generally speaking, we advise having no more than two team owners.

Any more than this will probably cause misunderstandings and annoyance. To ensure that everyone is on the same page, team owners should always communicate closely with one another. This is especially important while setting things up, which is covered later in this chapter. In order to know where to turn for initial support and inquiries, team members must constantly be aware of who the team owners are.

MEMBER OF THE TEAM

Members of a team may belong to one or more teams. Any employee at a company with a Teams license can join the team. It is the duty of team members to remain up to date on their work. They are in charge of talking about and creating content that is suitable for the team and channel. For their notifications to be effective, they must also know how to follow and favorite teams and channels.

127

REVIEW OF FEATURES

It's amazing how much of Microsoft Teams' features can be altered and personalized. While some feature modification is carried out at the organizational level, others are done at the team level. In the team settings, team owners can alter member rights and the features of their team. Selecting and training the proper team owners is crucial for another reason: they have enormous influence on the user experience.

Office 365 administrators can modify and personalize the functionality for every team by using tenant-wide settings. There are some options that can be adjusted at both the organizational and team levels. Recognizing that the tenant-wide settings always take precedence over the team settings is crucial.

Take note: Although Teams features can be customized at both the organizational and team levels, organizational settings are always prioritized.

SETTINGS IN ORGANIZATIONS

Tenant-wide Office 365 admin center settings can be used to adjust an organization's Teams experience and features. Every company has different business requirements and situations. Because of the way Teams is designed, a large portion of its functionality may be turned on or off as needed.

128

An organization can determine which functionalities should be enabled or disabled by conducting a pilot. Everyone in the company becomes used to Teams' features after it is made available to everyone. If things are taken away after end customers have begun utilizing them, they will be unhappy. Because of this, it is crucial that Teams administrators evaluate the Office 365 admin center's feature settings.

To examine the admin center's Teams tenant-wide settings

- Select Settings and then Services & add-ins.
- From the options, choose Microsoft Teams.

Microsoft offers a way to disable or limit email integration because by default, each channel is assigned an email address that anyone can send emails to. Office 365 administrators can prevent anyone from emailing all channels, or they can set it so that only individuals from specific email domains can send channel emails. We advise against disabling email to any channel unless absolutely necessary. When emails are sent to the channel email address, they appear as messages in the conversations tab, where team members can reply, which minimizes the number of group emails. If you start receiving spam or emails become distracting or irrelevant to your work, you may want to limit who can email the channel.

Jason Taylor

∧ Email integration

Allow users to send email to channels   ▮▮▯ On

Allow senders list (separated each domain with a comma)

contoso.net,microsoft.com

131

CHAPTER SEVEN

CLOUD STORAGE AND EXTERNAL APPS

It is possible for Microsoft Teams to integrate with other applications. Users can work with these apps without ever leaving the Microsoft Teams app by selecting them when establishing tabs in channels. Additionally, they have discretion over which apps are permitted. Apps that load from the side can also be enabled.

∧ Apps

Enable default apps

✓ Name	∧
✓ Bing News	
✓ Dynamics 365	
✓ Flow	
✓ Forms	
✓ Images	
✓ News	∨

Allow external apps in Microsoft Teams   ▇▇▇▎ On

Allow sideloading of external apps   ▇▇▇▎ On

Enable new external apps by default   ▇▇▇▎ On

132

CLOUD-BASED STORAGE

It is possible to set up cloud storage services like Dropbox or Google Drive that are not part of Office 365 to enable file sharing and uploading. Office 365 administrators have the choice to keep some cloud storage features enabled or to disable all of them.

∧ Custom cloud storage	
Box	▬▮ On
Dropbox	▬▮ On
Google Drive	▬▮ On
ShareFile	▬▮ On

MESSAGES

The Office 365 administrator has the ability to modify a wide range of message settings. It is possible to fully disable private chat. Memes, stickers, and GIFs can be changed to personalize the chat experience. If uploading explicit content raises concerns, the content rating can be altered. Editing and deleting messages is influenced by the main messaging settings. Users have the ability to edit and remove all of their own messages by default. Team owners have the option to remove all messages, albeit this feature is not activated by

133

default. If a team receives a lot of "fluff" communications, it could be necessary to activate this. Team owners should be trained and given direction on how to use this parameter, which should be enabled carefully.

MEETINGS AND CALLS

It is possible to disable ad hoc, private, and channel meetings. on order to prevent confusion, it could be a good idea to disable meetings on Teams if an organization already has a virtual meeting approach that users have accepted and it is effective. If there are bandwidth or security regulations that forbid it, a company may have trouble allowing screen sharing and video during meetings. Another option that can be turned off if needed is private calling.

⌃ Calls and meetings

Allow scheduling for private meetings	On
Allow ad-hoc channel meetup	On
Allow scheduling for channel meetings	On
Allow videos in meetings	On
Allow screen sharing in meetings	On
Allow private calling	On

EXTERNAL USERS

Teams facilitates collaboration between team members and external users. Inviting clients, subcontractors, vendors, and consultants to view team files and participate in discussions within Teams is a typical business necessity. Allowing

Settings by user/license type

Select the user/license type you want to configure — Guest ▾

Turn Microsoft Teams on or off for all users of this type — Off

135

external users in Teams raises privacy problems for many agencies. Office 365 administrators can choose Guest as the license type and then disable Teams for users of that kind in order to prevent external users from using Teams.

TEAM-LEVEL CONFIGURATIONS

By altering the team settings, team owners can personalize how their team is utilized. Changes can be made to team member and visitor rights, mention teams and channels, and access "fun" options like GIFs, memes, and emoticons. No other teams are affected by these parameters.

Team members should be aware that they should only alter these settings when absolutely necessary. To ensure that end users are not taken aback when they are unable to do a task, team owners should notify them of any changes to the settings.

HOW TO EXAMINE THE TEAM'S CONFIGURATION

- To the right of the team name, click the ellipse (...).
- Select Manage team.
- Select Settings.

Members   Channels   Settings   Apps

› **Team picture** — Add a team picture

› **Member permissions** — Enable channel creation, adding apps, and more

› **Guest permissions** — Enable channel creation

› **@mentions** — Choose who can use @team and @channel mentions

› **Fun stuff** — Allow emoji, memes, GIFs, or stickers

137

PERMISSIONS FOR MEMBERS

Members of a team can have their permissions removed by the team owner.

All team members have their permissions configured. With the exception of guests, it is impossible to give some team members different permissions than others. We advise removing the ability to add, edit, remove, and restore channels, applications, tabs, and connectors for big or less tech-savvy teams.

The team owner should decide whether or not to carry out these tasks. Team members' ability to modify and/or remove communications may be restricted by certain organizations. When adjusting these settings, exercise extreme caution because team members will be considerably less inclined to utilize Teams' discussion feature if they are aware that they cannot correct errors or remove messages that they later decide they no longer want to use.

PERMISSIONS FOR VISITORS

Permissions to create, edit, and remove channels can be granted to guest team members. This is turned off by default as there aren't many circumstances in which visitors should or require this control.

INTEGRATION OF EMAIL

To allow team members or email addresses to email the channel address, it is feasible to limit access to specific domains. Email settings should only be changed for specific business purposes because changing them for just a few channels confuses end users.

MENTIONS OF THE TEAM AND CHANNEL

both channels and teams can be brought up in discussions. The primary function of mentions is to initiate notifications. When a team is mentioned, all team members receive notifications. Notifications are sent to all channel followers when a channel is mentioned. Teams is frequently criticized for having too many notifications, which causes users to lose interest in them. If team members are getting too many notifications, the team owner might wish to turn off team and channel mentions.

Bots are started via chat messages or conversation messages in channels in Microsoft Teams, albeit the type of bot installed may only function in one of these scenarios. Typically, a bot will respond with details about its capabilities when you give it a message. Other features, including a tool that may be used in a tab, are included in some of the programs.

@mentions

Choose who can use @team and @channel mentions

Allow @team or @[team name] mentions (this will send a notification to everyone on the team)

Allow @channel or @[channel name] mentions (this will send a notification to everyone who has favorited the channel being mentioned)

SETTINGS FOR MEMES, GIFS, AND STICKERS

141

The team owner has the ability to disable stickers, GIFs, and memes. To get rid of anything unsuitable, team owners can also create a content filter. If there are guests who are clients or customers, team owners might want to turn off the "fun stuff". Additionally, the team may have to disable memes, GIFs, and stickers entirely if they are being used excessively and they don't follow the team owner's advice to use them less.

In brief

We went over some best practices and questions to ask when a new team is needed in this chapter. As you can see, an effective Microsoft Teams launch requires careful consideration of a number of factors. The good news is that each corresponding team should function more smoothly and have a higher likelihood of adoption after you have taken the time to put this up. In the upcoming chapter, we go over how your company can use Teams to further automate business operations with bots and Microsoft Flow.

TEAM BUSINESS PROCESS AUTOMATION

Business procedures and information collection are increasingly becoming automated in the modern workplace. Business process automation is probably an excellent option for repetitive, routine, and uncomplicated tasks at work that need data entry or information seeking. Since Microsoft Teams is a digital workspace designed to foster creativity, communication, teamwork, and decision-making, it makes sense to automate as many activities as you can, freeing up time to concentrate on leading the team to greater success. Because Microsoft Teams makes it possible to use data from other cloud-based apps, there are a lot of opportunities for business process automation. Microsoft Flow and bots can be used in Microsoft Teams to automate business processes.

BOTS: WHAT ARE THEY?

Given that Microsoft Teams is a chat-based program, it should come as no surprise that using a chatbot to automate certain business procedures is possible. A bot is a program designed to help end users automate and expedite activities by sending them pre-programmed messages and choice prompts. Depending on the deployed bot, Microsoft Teams provides a platform for team members to engage with intelligent bots through both natural chat discussions and specialized commands. Microsoft Teams bots establish connections with cloud services. Generally speaking, bots are designed to execute repetitive, easy activities far more quickly than a human could. Microsoft Teams bots establish connections with cloud services. The Microsoft Bot

143

144

Framework is used by developers to create them, making it simple for them to interact with the App Store and Microsoft Teams. Bots are started via chat messages or conversation messages in channels in Microsoft Teams, albeit the type of bot installed may only function in one of these scenarios. Typically, a bot will respond with details about its capabilities when you give it a message. Other features, including a tool that may be used in a tab, are included in some of the programs.

THE CAPABILITIES OF BOTS

You can interact with the T-Bot, a bot included with Microsoft Teams, to obtain information. T-Bot provides a message with instructions on how to use Teams when it is first opened. The T-Bot is an excellent illustration of the functionality and capabilities of Microsoft Teams bots.

Microsoft Teams bots link users to cloud services, then use the capabilities of those cloud services to carry out routine tasks in Teams when you communicate with them and give them instructions. Bots assist Microsoft Teams users with tasks including managing team tasks, arranging meetings or events, and conducting polls to get input from team required to automate your company's process. If not, it could be required to install and merge the capabilities of two or more bots

146

The three primary tasks that bots are carrying out are scheduling, task management, and polling, despite the fact that apps in the Microsoft Teams store are categorized into the following areas: Analytics and BI, Developer and IT, Education, Human Resources, Productivity, Project Management, Sales and Support, and Social and Fun.

Store

Search all

All

Apps
Bots
Tabs
Connectors
Messaging

Top picks
Analytics and BI
Developer and IT
Education
Human resources
Productivity
Project management
Sales and support
Social and fun

147

MAKING A SCHEDULE

Team bots can help in the time-consuming task of meeting scheduling. Bots can schedule meetings by syncing team members' calendars and displaying available times, polling attendees to determine the best time to meet, scheduling meetings and sending out invitations, and even offering a list of available meeting rooms for booking. We are aware that Teams can host meetings, but certain companies that utilize alternative meeting software can turn this feature off. Team members can create meetings in these services by using the bots that are available in many popular meeting services.

MANAGING TASKS

Project managers can use Microsoft Teams bots to help with activities like gathering team members' daily progress reports. A bot can automatically send out reminders to complete status reports. Team members can then reply with their current status, which is added to a report that the project manager can view. It is possible to set up reminders for team members according to their due dates. Additionally, there are bots that can monitor and control the life cycles of tasks and documents. A bot can also be used in Microsoft Teams to track time based on tasks. Bots can be used to automate project management business operations that include data collection, tracking, and reminders.

148

SURVEYING

Microsoft Teams contains bots with polling capabilities. By giving team members, a predetermined selection of options from which to choose, polling is an easy method of gathering their input. When a new poll is created in Microsoft Teams, team members can receive an automatic notification. By combining the responses, the bot makes it possible to examine the outcomes. Although this functionality may seem minor, it may be highly powerful and a big time-saver when trying to seek the opinions of team members when reaching a choice.

HOW TO ADD BOTS

Bots can be added to a team by every team member unless the configuration is altered by either the Office 365 administrator or the team owner.

Note: External apps can be blocked by the Office 365 administrator. If you cannot add a bot, this could be the issue.

How To add a bot to a team

- Click the ellipse (…) to the right of the team that you wish to add the bot to.
- Select Manage team.
- Select Apps.
- Press the button labeled "Go to Store."

149

- To display just the bot apps, click bots on the left under Store.

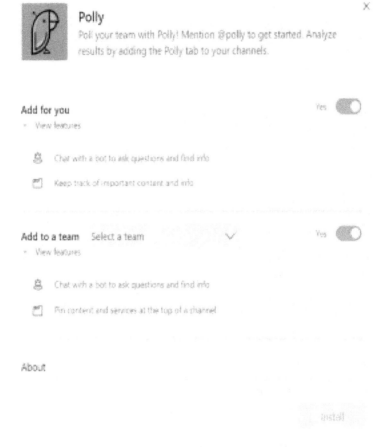

- Decide which bot to include on the squad.
- Click Install after choosing the Team name from the Add to team drop-down box.

150

USING TEAMS WITH MICROSOFT FLOW

As part of Office 365, Microsoft Flow is a cloud-based program that is available for free when purchased with Microsoft Teams. Data collection, approval automation, file copying, notice sending, and more are all possible with Microsoft Flow, a business process automation application. Data from Microsoft Teams can be linked with data from other Office 365 programs and external cloud-based apps using Microsoft Flow.

A flow must be activated in order to operate. The creation or modification of an item in SharePoint, the submission of a new Microsoft Forms answer, or the addition, updating, or deletion of an Office 365 Outlook event are just a few instances of the numerous triggers that originate from hundreds of apps. Although Microsoft Flow capability is constantly evolving, there are currently no Microsoft Teams triggers. Conditions that permit various outcomes depending on whether they are true or not can be inserted once a flow has been initiated. The tasks that the flow completes are called actions. The flow completes the business process through actions.

151

TEAMS ACTIONS IN MICROSOFT FLOW

There are four actions that Microsoft Flow conducts in Microsoft Teams. These actions give an automatic way to create a channel, list the channels, list teams, and post messages.

Triggers (0)   Actions (4)

🔳 Microsoft Teams - Create a channel

🔳 Microsoft Teams - List channels

🔳 Microsoft Teams - List teams

🔳 Microsoft Teams - Post message

ESTABLISH A CHANNEL

One very helpful feature in Microsoft Teams is the create a channel action. In response to a trigger, this action automatically establishes a channel. For instance, you may design a flow that is initiated when an item is added to a SharePoint list by using a property from a previous phase as the channel name. Using the Title field from the SharePoint item as the channel name, it then creates a channel. The flow can be modified to include a phase that would only permit

152

the creation of a channel with permission from a higher authority, such the team owner or an IT specialist. A list of a team's channels is automatically generated by the list channels action. It keeps an eye on channel creation; for instance, to ensure that no channels are being formed improperly, an IT department can be sent a weekly list of all channels. The flow can be modified to only list channels that were formed during a specific number of days by adding a condition.

List teams (Preview)

No additional information is needed for this step. You will be able to use the outputs in subsequent steps.

153

ENUMERATE TEAMS

Similar to the list channels action, the list teams action lists the teams rather than the channels. This is a fantastic method for automating the process of keeping an eye on the teams that have been established within an Office 365 tenant. An email or report can include the Team name, Team ID, and Team description properties. The list only includes the teams that the user executing the flow is a member of.

SEND A MESSAGE

The most often used Microsoft Teams action in Microsoft Flow is probably the post a message action. When anything noteworthy occurs outside of Microsoft Teams, it alerts a

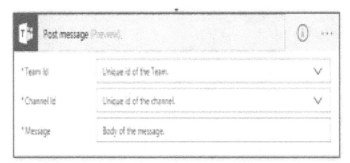

team. When a task in SharePoint is marked as completed, a new form is submitted, or a bug is opened in Visual Studio Team Services, it is common practice to broadcast a message to a team channel.

154

TEMPLATES

A number of prebuilt templates are available in Microsoft Flow. Templates are the most straightforward approach to begin using Microsoft Flow and require very little setting. You can search for teams to obtain a list of all the templates that integrate with Microsoft Teams. Any other service that the flow connects to requires an account, and in order for it to function, you must supply credentials. Steps and conditions can be added after using Microsoft Flow templates as a starting point.

TEAMS' MICROSOFT FLOW APP

A chatbot is offered by the Microsoft Flow software, which may be installed in Microsoft Teams. Users can monitor their flows with the use of this unique app. Teams allows for the creation and editing of flows. Other team members cannot see the Microsoft Flow app because it is a personal app. After installing the Microsoft Flow app, each user may see their approvals and processes. Flows are executed by command using the Microsoft Flow bot in Teams. The Microsoft Flow bot provides a list of available flows to execute when you chat with it. After that, you can tell it to execute a flow by typing Run flow and then the flow's number. Currently, the Microsoft Flow bot only starts scheduled flows. You may use the Microsoft Flow bot to provide the report on demand as needed in Teams if you set up a scheduled flow that identifies every channel in a team and sends it in a monthly report. Another situation is that you can use the Microsoft Flow bot to post on demand if you have a scheduled flow that consistently publishes articles, links to websites, or messages to social networking platforms like LinkedIn or Twitter.

157

CONCLUSION

As we wrap up our comprehensive exploration of Microsoft Teams, it's evident that this powerful collaboration platform has fundamentally reshaped the landscape of communication and teamwork within organizations. In a world where remote work and digital collaboration have transitioned from a novelty to a necessity, Teams stands out as a holistic solution that integrates the diverse tools and functionalities essential for effective collaboration, regardless of where team members are located.

Throughout this book, we have journeyed through the myriad of features that Microsoft Teams offers. From its robust communication capabilities to its seamless integration with Microsoft 365 applications, Teams provides a versatile environment that empowers users to connect, collaborate, and create. We've examined how Teams facilitates real-time communication through various channels, including instant messaging, voice calls, and video conferencing. The ability to engage in spontaneous conversations or conduct formal meetings with ease is crucial in today's fast-paced work environment.

Moreover, the collaborative features within Teams allow for enhanced teamwork and collective problem-solving. The ability to co-author documents in real time, share files effortlessly, and manage projects using integrated tools such as Planner and OneNote are game changers for productivity. By creating dedicated channels for specific projects or topics, teams can streamline their discussions and keep relevant information organized. This not only reduces clutter but also ensures that everyone is aligned and informed.

One of the standout aspects of Microsoft Teams is its customization capabilities. Teams can be tailored to fit the unique workflows and preferences of individual organizations. The integration of third-party applications and bots allows teams to enhance their functionality further, adapting the platform to meet specific needs. Whether it's incorporating tools for project management, customer relationship management, or analytics, Teams can serve as the central hub for all collaborative efforts.

Fostering Team Culture

In addition to its technical capabilities, Microsoft Teams plays a vital role in fostering a strong team culture. The importance of maintaining a sense of community cannot be overstated, especially in remote or hybrid work settings.

Teams provides numerous opportunities for social interaction, allowing members to connect on a personal level. Features like polls, announcements, and fun integrations, such as GIFs and stickers, can help create a more engaging and enjoyable work environment.

A positive team culture is essential for morale, motivation, and overall job satisfaction. By utilizing the social features in Teams, organizations can cultivate an environment where employees feel valued, included, and connected. Regular check-ins, virtual team-building activities, and recognition of achievements can all contribute to a cohesive team spirit, even from a distance.

Security and Compliance

As organizations increasingly rely on digital collaboration tools, the importance of security and compliance cannot be overlooked. Microsoft Teams is built with robust security features designed to protect sensitive information and ensure compliance with industry regulations. From data encryption to multi-factor authentication, Teams provides the necessary safeguards to maintain the integrity of your organization's communications.

160

This focus on security gives teams the confidence to collaborate openly without the fear of compromising their data. Organizations can trust that their information is secure, allowing them to focus on what truly matters: achieving their goals and driving success.

The Journey Ahead

As you move forward with Microsoft Teams, it's crucial to remember that the true power of this platform lies not only in its features but also in the way you and your team choose to utilize them. Embrace a culture of collaboration, encourage open communication, and leverage the tools at your disposal to create a dynamic and productive work environment.

In this rapidly evolving landscape, staying adaptable and willing to learn is key. As Microsoft Teams continues to evolve, new features and updates will emerge, providing even more opportunities for enhanced collaboration. Stay informed about these changes and be open to experimenting with new functionalities that can further streamline your workflows.

Final Thoughts

161

Ultimately, Microsoft Teams is not just a tool; it's a transformative platform that empowers teams to work smarter together. By embracing its capabilities, you can enhance communication, streamline workflows, and drive better outcomes for your organization. This journey is about more than just mastering a software application; it's about fostering an environment where collaboration thrives, creativity flourishes, and teams can achieve their collective potential.

We hope this book has provided you with valuable insights and practical strategies to make the most of Microsoft Teams. With the right mindset and approach, you can unlock the full potential of this platform, paving the way for innovation, productivity, and success within your organization.

Here's to your continued growth and success as you harness the power of Microsoft Teams to transform the way you and your team collaborate, communicate, and create together. The possibilities are endless, and the future of work is bright with Microsoft Teams at your side.

NOTE